Baby Blue
Marble

❑ ■ ❑

Baby Blue Marble

□ ■ □

by
Cynthia Lanning

BRISTOL
BOOKS

Library of Congress Card Number: 89-60525
ISBN: 0-917851-33-1
Recommended Dewey Decimal Classification: 813.52

BRISTOL BOOKS
An imprint of Good News, A Forum for Scriptural Christianity, Inc.
308 East Main Street • Wilmore, Kentucky 40390

□

Dedicated to my son,
John Kenneth Lanning
Our quest for you made this book possible.

□

Contents

◻ ■ ◻

◻ ■ ◻

Chapter 1

A Tale of Two Meals

□ ■ □

Laura realized it was time for another cup of coffee, the third of the morning. J. D. had just plopped another stack of page proofs on her desk, gleefully reminding her that the product was already two weeks behind schedule.

Laura shrugged her slender shoulders and pulled the huge pile of paper toward her. Her shoulder length, light brown hair fell over the thick, paper-clipped chapters as her clear blue eyes scanned the typeset copy for obvious errors. She wrinkled her nose in disgust as she noticed several problems even at first glance. It was definitely time for that third cup of coffee.

One of the most disillusioning things about publishing, Laura thought as she scanned her crowded desk for her coffee mug, *is that we're creating products, not books.* At Northwest Press, employees didn't refer to books by titles—which were usually long and technical—but by stock numbers. The menacing pile on her desk was called D-44 and had something to do with cost accounting.

Laura found her mug, a large ceramic one covered with colorful balloons, and decided she could use it a few more times before washing it. Feeling a hundred years old instead of only thirty, she slowly pushed herself away from her desk and shuffled to the break area.

"Good morning, Laura," said a cheerful, masculine voice behind her as she stood at the coffee maker.

"Hello, Andrew."

"Hope you slept well," he said, pouring himself a cup of coffee.

"It was without you, wasn't it?" Laura immediately regretted her comment, which changed the tone of their conversation from cool and cordial to hateful and intimate.

"Laura, we really need to talk about it. About us. Why don't you meet me for lunch?"

Incredibly, she heard herself say, "Okay."

"I'll stop by your desk at noon."

He took his coffee and left. Hers was growing cold.

Later that morning Elaine stopped by Laura's desk. "How many times have you told him it's over? It's been almost two years since you told him to forget it. I don't understand why you can never say no to that man."

"Neither do I. I guess I keep wanting to put that situation neatly behind me. I always want to leave with good feelings."

"You sound more like a Care Bear than a human being. He's a creep and a cad, and you'll just have to leave it at that."

"I know."

□

When noon and Andrew arrived, Laura had barely dented the stack of page proofs. "I can only take a quick break. We're really behind on D-44," she told him.

"Well, we'll just grab a bite in the cafeteria," Andrew suggested while putting on his Brooks Brothers blue blazer and adjusting his lapels. *Andrew would make a perfect secret agent,* Laura thought as she pulled her purse from the back of her desk drawer. *He's so nondescript, the kind of person you wouldn't remember if you passed him on the street.* Andrew was running a comb through his not too thin, not too thick medium brown hair. He was neither

tall nor short, fat nor thin. His eyes sometimes looked
brown and sometimes muddy green, depending on the
light. His face was very normal; his chin neither
prominent nor weak, eyebrows neither thin nor bushy. His
only remarkable characteristic was the distracted, self-con-
tented way he usually held his face.

Laura had promised herself she would never endure
another lunch under the real or imagined stares of gossip-
ing co-workers. "What about Theo's?" she suggested.

But that was a mistake, too. Theo's was more private,
but the little sandwich shop was not unknown to
Northwest employees. If spotted there, the tryst would
seem even less innocent. Her brain was tired of having to
think of all the angles.

"Sounds great," said Andrew.

They reached Northwest's heavy glass front door
together, but Laura surged ahead and opened it briskly for
herself.

They drove the five blocks to Theo's in her blue Honda
Accord. When she turned on the ignition, the radio began
blaring an Amy Grant song. Laura quickly turned it off.

For some reason, Theo's ancient marble counters and
high pressed tin ceilings always reminded Laura of a
chapel. The cracked terrazzo floor was identical to the
floor of the church she had attended throughout childhood.
Paddle fans labored above, their whirring creating a
hushed atmosphere in the narrow shop no matter how
many people wandered in for thick sandwiches or hand-
dipped ice cream.

A shuffling, elderly waitress appeared. Andrew ordered
Laura's favorites without consulting her—roast beef and
swiss on wheat and a raspberry soda. "You seem
depressed, Laura," he observed in a fatherly tone.

"It's just the usual story. Too much work, too little time,"
Laura sighed. "It doesn't take any deep psychoanalyzing to
figure out what's wrong with me."

Andrew smiled, admiring her eyes as she avoided his by
studying the floral design in the small shop's wallpaper.

Her blue eyes were an unexpected surprise under her glossy brown hair, which she wore in a sophisticated but sensible shoulder length style. She was not strikingly beautiful; heads didn't turn when she walked into a room. But her healthy, well-scrubbed good looks and self-effacing charm made her the kind of woman people found increasingly attractive as they got to know her.

"Are you and Peter having any luck getting pregnant?"

"That's really none of your business."

"You used to enjoy telling me your business."

The food came. Laura's midwestern appetite never failed her, and she ate as though she were fueling her Honda.

"Andrew, I only agreed to meet you today to try to finally give some closure to our relationship," said Laura as she finished her soda. "I don't bear you any ill will. In fact, I feel terrible because I have caused you pain. But you knew I was married when we started. I never made you any promises. It's been almost two years since we . . . had our thing."

"What do you want, Laura? I just want to know what you want."

"Why do you have to keep asking me that? I want you to stay out of my life, as I've told you a zillion times. I'm pulling my marriage back together and I don't need you in my life. After everything that's happened, we can never be just friends."

"You call what you have a marriage . . . ?"

"Why do you always presume to know what's right for me? When I was thinking about leaving Peter you encouraged me to make my own decisions and not listen to him. But now that I'm making my own choices, and they aren't what you want, you try to tell me how to run my life. How dare you tell me what my marriage is like! How would you even know what makes a good or bad marriage?"

"I can't understand the hold that man has on you. You two have nothing in common."

Laura was chewing her sandwich and couldn't respond.
"I just want you to be happy, Laura."
"Then leave me alone."
Andrew looked as though an electric shock had passed
through his body. His eyes narrowed. Laura had never
seen him look that way.
"Fine. If that's what you want, that's what you'll get."
They ate the rest of the meal in silence.

□

Back at the office, the situation was deteriorating. J. D.
had left a note on her desk. Clutching it like a summons,
Laura knocked on his door.

As a senior editor, J. D., a large, bald man who wore
sweater vests and reading glasses, merited a private office
instead of one of the partitioned cubbyholes where Laura
and most of the other employees at Northwest toiled. He
had reached the stage in his career where, because of his
reputation as an expert, just having his name on the title
page of a textbook could sway a state's textbook adoption
committee in that product's favor. Therefore, Northwest
could afford to pay him extravagantly for very little work.
The only days Laura knew him to arrive at the office on
time were snowy mornings when he'd rise unspeakably
early to get there before everyone else. Then he would
loiter by the coffee maker all morning and crow about
other people's lack of dedication.

"Laura, I'm concerned about D-44," J. D. said as he
gazed out his huge windows at the car wash across the
street. "I know we moved the deadline up, but we had no
choice after marketing discovered the Texas adoption committee is meeting in two months."

"Well, it's in page proofs now. We're on the home
stretch."

"I'd like you to have that ready to go back for corrections
by Monday."

"But this is Thursday."

"Precisely."

Back at her desk, Laura's phone was blinking. It was
Elaine.

"Hey, lady, how's it going?"

"J. D. just cancelled my weekend."

"How nice of him. Why don't you come over for dinner
tonight? Nothing fancy. Tim has the kids. I have a business proposition I'd like to discuss with you."

"I'd love to. Peter's meeting a client tonight, and I'm in
no mood to sit at home alone. What time?"

"About seven o'clock."

"See you then."

□

Elaine was a tiny woman with curly red hair and the
milky way of freckles splashed across her face. She wore
lace collars and deep forest green and wine colored clothes.
Although she would have preferred to live in a Victorian
townhouse—and, having worked at Northwest for fourteen years, could probably afford one—as a divorced
mother of two young children she had neither the time nor
the energy for anything other than a trim suburban split
level in a good school district.

"Greetings. Well, how was lunch with Andrew?" Elaine
asked as she took Laura's jacket.

"Oh, nothing exciting. I asked him to leave me alone for
the millionth time, and he said he would. I didn't leave
with any warm fuzzy feelings, though."

"What could you expect? Like most men, he's selfish. It's
fine for them to dump a woman, but if they lose the battle
of love, watch out. Men would rather shoot you than stare
sorrowfully at your photograph for hours, the way a normal heartbroken woman would."

"Well, he did drive by our house and yell at us out of his
car window once."

"You were smart to have an affair with a yuppie. Yuppie
men aren't the shotgun type."

"Peter grabbed a hammer and ran out into the street.
He dented the rear of Andrew's Jetta as he drove away. I

don't know what Peter would have done with the hammer if Andrew hadn't left. Just a primal reflex, I guess."

"Men have a lot of those."

"Actually, I think that bizarre little incident helped Peter and me stay together. We were facing a common enemy. I stood on the porch crying while Peter defended his castle."

"Sounds medieval, just like Peter."

"He tries hard. We really are getting our marriage back together."

"Are you two in therapy?"

"We talked about it, but we're just too busy. J. D. has been pushing me hard. I almost always bring home a bulging briefcase. And being in sales, Peter never knows what his schedule will be from one day to the next. We were afraid making time to go to therapy would just put more strain on us."

Elaine was making omelets, not just plain omelets, but fluffy ones filled with various cheeses and mushrooms. She was also throwing together a lettuce salad with mandarin oranges and almonds in a vinegar dressing.

"That brings me to the business proposition I mentioned," she said while pouring hot tea into gilt-edged china cups.

"I'm all ears."

"How would you like to help me start a new business?"

"Are you serious?"

"I certainly am. In fact, after dinner I'll show you how I've redone my basement into a computer room. I've already bought most of the equipment for a desktop publishing business."

"After eight years, I'd do anything to get out of Northwest. I mean, I'll have to discuss this with Peter. But, basically, when do I start?"

□

That next Monday morning, Laura plopped her resignation on J. D.'s desk along with the stack of finished page

proofs. As she left his empty office (as usual, he was not
there yet), Laura told herself, *after eight years of bondage
at Northwest, I'm free at last, free at last.*

News of Elaine's and her resignations flew through the
company in less time than it takes to format a floppy disk.
By eleven-thirty, three people had called and four had
stopped by Laura's desk to confirm the rumor. Around
noon, her interoffice line was blinking again.

"Laura Morton speaking."

"Laura, this is Andrew."

"Oh. I thought we were going to leave each other alone."

"I'm just calling to make sure you aren't leaving
Northwest because of me. I don't want to destroy your life."

"Why do you think my every decision has something to
do with you? Working for Elaine is a better opportunity, a
chance to get in on the ground floor of something that
could be really big."

"But I know you, Laura. You're not the risk taking type.
Her new business could belly up in six months, and then
where would you be? You've got a specialized skill in a
small city with few other places to peddle it. And I don't
think you'd want to come crawling back to Northwest."

"Elaine's been in this field almost eighteen years. She
has all kinds of contacts with publishers in other cities. I
think she has excellent prospects."

"Yes, but Elaine is, well . . . "

"You never liked her because she sees right through
you."

"She thinks she sees right through everyone. I'm being
objective now. I just don't think she has what it takes to
make it in the world of business."

"And how would you know what it takes to make it on
your own in business?" Laura replied, surprised at how
rude she could be with Andrew.

"I still care about you, Laura. I'm concerned about your
best interests," he replied, ignoring her contemptuous tone
as though she were a child who couldn't be held respon-
sible for what she said.

"I'll be honest with you, Andrew. I'm not taking this new job to get away from you, but that is something I'm looking forward to. Won't you ever leave me alone?"

"I'll always be a part of your life. What we shared was very special. You can't change that now, Laura."

"What we shared was wrong. I feel terrible about it. It was the worst and ugliest thing I have ever done in my life." Laura fervently hoped no one was eavesdropping on either end of this conversation.

"It was beautiful, and you know it. Your antique, repressive religious ideas keep you from acknowledging that. Someday you'll wake up and remember how wonderful our relationship was. I just hope for your sake that I'm still around when that happens."

"You are unbelievable. My religious beliefs make me very happy. I'd be even happier if I'd never ignored them by getting mixed up with you."

"You know where to find me when you want me," Andrew said as he quickly hung up.

He just won't let this horrible episode of my life end, thought Laura. *This is like having emotional AIDS. If only I could undo everything. I never meant to have an affair. I'm supposed to be a Christian.*

The mental self-lashing continued as Laura dug a brown paper bag out of her bottom desk drawer. She had packed her lunch to avoid the interrogation she would surely face if she ate in the employee cafeteria that day.

As she ate her tuna fish without tasting it, Laura remembered how they had met. Andrew had been loaned from another department to help her meet some unrealistic deadline. They began working through lunch, carting massive printouts to the cafeteria.

One day, Andrew suggested they reserve one of the conference rooms till the project was done so they would not have to gather it up to journey to the cafeteria or each other's desks.

As they worked together in the silent, carpeted room, they began talking about their lives. Laura didn't know ex-

actly when the affair began. At no point did she say to herself, *Well, now I think I will go ahead and have an affair.*
It crept up quietly, unannounced, like a stray cat that
hangs around the back door and eventually becomes a pet.
Had she stopped to make a conscious decision, she knew
what it would have been. She knew what adultery was.
She had grown up in a church, attended a Christian college and had once tearfully invited Christ into her heart at
an altar.

Although I didn't realize it at the time, I suppose the affair officially started the day Andrew held my hand, Laura
thought.

She and Peter had argued the night before, which was
especially traumatic because they seldom fought. Both had
grown up in homes filled with noisy quarrels and learned
to suppress their angry feelings for fear of causing conflict.
When Peter would cancel their plans at the last minute because of work, Laura would pretend not to mind. When
Laura would go to bed early for the third night in a row totally exhausted, Peter would hide the rejection he felt.
They secretly nursed their disappointments like embarrassing infections, sabotaging the very communication
needed to improve their marriage.

That particular morning, as Laura and Andrew spread
their printouts and artwork on the conference room table,
Andrew commented that Laura seemed depressed. To her
astonishment, Laura began pouring out her emotions in
an uncharacteristically unprofessional manner. Andrew
held her hand and listened without interrupting. When
she had finished, he concurred with her criticisms of Peter.
He couldn't understand why a man would foolishly destroy
a relationship with a wonderful woman like Laura by
being insensitive or egotistical.

*Now I realize the only reason he listened so understandingly was because he wasn't involved with me yet and
didn't have his own agenda to pursue,* Laura thought. *Yes,
I will certainly be glad to leave Northwest. I'll be free of
him, and maybe of some of my guilt, at last.*

Giants in the Promised Land

□ ■ □

"Elaine, what did you do with the Pratt manuscript?"
"I don't know. Look on the shelf over the copier."
"I thought we were going to keep all unedited
manuscripts in the blue filing cabinet."
"We started doing that, but some of them are on disk
and I've been putting them in the bin next to the Compaq."

Laura grumbled to herself as she searched for the
misplaced pile of papers. Every day Elaine had a new system. Supplies that were kept in a drawer would be moved
to a cupboard. Elaine would even rearrange office furniture, including Laura's desk, at night. But perhaps
Elaine's most irritating habit of all, from Laura's view-
point, was her tendency to leave the caps off ink pens.

Laura finally located the missing document, but scowled
as she read the note attached to it. "Elaine, how could you
promise University Press that we'd have the Pratt
manuscript ready in two weeks?"

"If I hadn't, we wouldn't have gotten the contract. When
we're better established we can start dictating customers'
deadlines. But for now we have to promise them the moon
to lure them away from our competitors."

"The moon I can understand, but this is Pluto!"

Laura felt a too familiar hot sensation on the back of
her neck. She knew that when the heat spread around her
neck and up to her cheeks, she would become a horrible
person.

"Elaine, why are we doing this? We're making less
money for working longer hours with no benefits. This is
crazy."

Elaine turned from her desk and replied, with no trace
of a smile, "Surely you didn't think we'd waltz into a multi-
million dollar business like fairy princesses! Life is hard.
But you don't know that. You floated from high school to
college to a nice little job at Northwest and never had any
lean years."

"And I suppose you've spent time in soup kitchens."

"It took me seven years to finish college because I was
married to a creep, had two babies, got cut off from my
family and worked minimum wage jobs to get through. We
ate pancakes or macaroni and cheese almost every night.
But in the end, it was worth it."

"Exactly. That's why I don't understand why you threw
away your job at Northwest for this."

"You still don't understand. People at Northwest are
taking a coffee break about now, getting paid for it,
making personal calls and getting paid for it. And yet
Northwest still makes huge profits. That means there's
money to be made in this business and I'm willing to
sacrifice for a few years to get it. I've sunk twenty-five
thousand dollars of my savings in this company. You work
for me; you haven't invested a dime. You're still thinking
like an employee."

"It's not like 'employee' is an obscene word."

"To me it is."

"Fine. That's great for you, but I'm getting tired of killing myself. It isn't worth it to me any more."

"If you want to quit, don't hang around for my sake.
Plenty of people at Northwest have drive and vision and
would love to get an opportunity like this."

"I'm not mad at you, Elaine. I know I underestimated

the sacrifice of starting a new business. I do want a great career, but I'm not willing to renounce everything else in my life to get it."

"I can understand where you're coming from, Laura. You're married to a workaholic, career-minded guy with a fantastic job. You know in the back of your mind that Peter's your safety net. If things don't work out, he'll bankroll you while you stay home and watch Phil Donahue and eat."

"That's not fair and you know it. I'm his fallback position, too. If he wanted to quit his job, I'd support him while he looked for another one. You're just in a different stage of life than I am. Sara and Rick are already in school. You're ready to forge ahead with your life while I'm hung up, hoping each month will be *the month.* My whole life is on hold while I wait for a baby I may never have."

"I wish you'd thought of all this before you committed yourself to my business," said Elaine, slamming a stack of papers on her desk.

Deciding to end the conversation before she said something regrettable, Laura sighed and lugged the Pratt manuscript to her desk. Elaine turned back to her work, and the only sound in the office was the low murmur of WXTZ on Elaine's radio. Listening to schlock music while working was another of Elaine's bad habits.

Unable to concentrate, Laura began mentally rehashing the details of her affair with Andrew for the millionth time. Whenever it was unoccupied, her mind was almost involuntarily drawn to this distasteful subject.

I did try to nip the relationship in the bud, Laura reminded herself. *I can't remember how many times I drove to work thinking, "Today is the day I end this thing once and for all." But I always lost my nerve when I'd get alone with him in the conference room.* He would be in some particularly needy state, or extremely affectionate and loving, or insistent that she give the relationship "one more chance."

As the affair progressed from hand holding to emotional

embraces to kissing to outright sex, Laura discovered that
Andrew was a mere mortal after all. He confided his heart-
aches to her, including details of a disastrous cohabitation
with a woman he met several years ago through a personal ad in the *Mother Earth News*. That relationship
ended when the woman left him for a job in another state,
taking with her a daughter they had accidentally
produced and whom Andrew seldom saw. Laura em-
pathized with Andrew's pain at being separated from his
only child. More than once, this heart-wrenching situation
kept her from ending their liaison. She sensed she was
helping him greatly by allowing him to talk about this personal tragedy.

They began meeting after work in city parks and out-of-
the-way restaurants, to "talk about us." Ironically, Laura
had been attracted to Andrew because he represented
freedom from the problems of her marriage, only to discover that he made just as many demands on her emotional energy as Peter.

As difficult as it is working for Elaine, Laura thought, *it
is so wonderful not to have to worry about running into
Andrew every time I leave my desk.*

□

As a few more weary weeks passed, Laura found Elaine
to be even more unreasonable than J. D. At Northwest, the
two women had been comrades. Now Elaine was the
enemy who invaded Laura's weekends.

"You know, Elaine," said Laura teasingly one chilly but
sunny early spring afternoon as she straightened a huge
stack of galleys on her desk, "if I didn't know and respect
you more, I'd swear you take advantage of our friendship
to get me to work longer hours."

"You know, Laura," Elaine shot back from her desk
across the room, "if I didn't know you better, I'd think you
were presuming on our friendship to always want time off."

"What time off?"

"Well, you balked at working last weekend to meet the Halcyon Press deadline."

"I balked because Peter and I had made plans to visit his family in Indiana, and we had to drop them at the last minute. Besides, I balked, but I came through for you."

"Yes, you did, and I appreciate it. You know how much Halcyon could mean to the business."

"Elaine, I want to talk to you about something when we're not super tired and under the gun for some deadline."

"When would that be?"

"Seriously, I don't want to leave you in a lurch, and this might be the best time since we only have one project in here now and you can handle it yourself."

"Laura, are you trying to tell me you're quitting?"

"I'm not sure."

"Let's be totally honest and not emotional about this. I thought you'd be the perfect person to help me get this business off the ground because you have always been so dedicated to your work. Half the people at Northwest are on an eternal coffee break, but you were different. You really busted your tail to get the work done. But I sense that you are at some sort of crisis point in your life right now."

"No, actually I'm not. Nothing is happening. Peter's job is going great. I'm working in the field I love. We're finally putting all that Andrew stuff behind us. Things couldn't be better."

"Then why did you bring this up?"

"I just don't know if I can continue to go at this pace. What if I do get pregnant? How could I keep this up? I just feel like there is no place in my life for *me*. I'm always letting Peter down because I don't have time for him any more. I don't know what's wrong. I just feel like I've lost control of my life, and I don't know how to get it back."

"So you're saying you want to quit."

"I think so."

"Look, we are between projects. Why don't you take some time off. If something comes in and you're not ready to come back, I have a couple of other people in mind who I think would be interested in working for me. It sounds like you need some time to sort things out."

"Are you sure you wouldn't despise me forever?"

"Of course not."

"You don't think I'm a wimp?"

"No. A wimp would avoid doing anything until she had a nervous breakdown and wound up hospitalized."

"I guess I'll finish going over these galleys and go home. Are you sure there aren't any hard feelings?"

"No, Care Bear. You can leave this situation with warm fuzzy feelings. I appreciate your being honest and not doing this when we had some horrible deadline breathing down our necks."

"I couldn't do that to you, Elaine."

"Besides, even if you do get pregnant, I know that a few weeks after you have the baby you'll go crazy at home. That's how women like us are. You'll be back. Besides, Peter will get tired of you waiting on him hand and foot."

"I don't want to wait on him, just maybe eat supper with him once a month."

"Well, don't spoil him."

□

Laura turned the key in the massive back door of their house as furtively as if she were a thief. It was two o'clock in the afternoon and the sun was beaming brightly on the tulips and iris planted around the foundation of their century-old, red brick home.

As Laura stepped into the kitchen, the sun was streaming through the windows in a way she seldom saw. She had intruded on the house's secret daytime life. Their two yellow tabby cats, Magic and Samantha, came rushing from their sleeping places, glad to see her, but confused.

As she laid her maroon leather briefcase on the kitchen table, Laura heard the mail plop through the mail slot by the front door. She checked the answering machine for calls; there were none. As she wandered to the front of the

house, each room she passed seemed possessed by an unfamiliar slumbering spirit. Passing through the living
room, which seemed bigger and quieter than usual, she
entered the foyer and scooped the mail from the floor. Two
bills, *Time* magazine, a brochure from the Discovery Center (Andrew had put her name on their mailing list and
was always encouraging her to attend various self-im-
provement seminars there) and their church's newsletter.

She peered through the curtains on the front door, draw-
ing them back as little as possible. Through the heavy
beveled glass she watched an elderly neighbor woman
across the street watering a sparse patch of flowers.
Meanwhile, a young woman in blue jeans pushed a rickety
stroller down the sidewalk, its wheels rasping sleepily and
cheerfully over the cement.

This is so odd, Laura thought. *Of course, life doesn't
cease around here while we are at work, waiting patiently
to resume when we walk through the door at night.*

She looked at her grandmother's antique tambour clock,
ticking loudly on the living room mantel. Peter wouldn't be
home for at least four hours.

Laura examined her options. It was too early to begin
dinner. No need to do any housework since Beulah had
just cleaned two days ago. Maybe she should tackle one of
the big projects she'd been putting off—cleaning out the
pantry, the garage or the basement. Perhaps she could
start refinishing the chest of drawers in the attic or scrap-
ing the peeling paint in the bathroom. Maybe she should
bake an elaborate dessert, the kind she made maybe once
a year, to surprise Peter. Or she could practice the piano—
she felt guilty for playing so seldom. "We're paying for
these lessons, young lady," still rang in her ears.

So many options. A magazine in a wicker basket next to
an overstuffed living room chair caught her eye. Maybe
she could read one article before starting some useful
project. She tossed her suit jacket on their carved antique
coffee table and loosened her silk bow tie. With a sigh, she
sank into the chair sideways, her shoulders resting on one

of the chair's plump arms and her legs dangling over the other. *I almost never sit here,* she thought. *I might as well thoroughly enjoy owning this chair for once. Otherwise, why have it?*

As she leafed through *Good Homemaking*, a magazine her mother gave her a gift subscription to each year, an article illustrated with a photograph of a woebegone middle-aged woman caught her eye: "How Your Husband's Affair Can Turn You Into a Divorce Statistic." The article reported the results of some study that found that eighty percent of all married men have affairs at some time during their marriages (*I don't think that means eighty percent of the men I know,* thought Laura). The article ended by listing ways women could "keep the sparkle in their marriages." These suggestions ranged from "experimenting with a more youthful hairstyle" to "surprising him by trying a new recipe you think he'll love."

Somehow, I don't think dowdy hairdos or boring dinner menus are causing the marital unrest in our nation thought Laura. *I suppose it goes without saying that one way to keep your man faithful is to avoid having an affair yourself. Funny they don't mention that here. But in a strange way, I think my affair actually helped keep our marriage intact. The guiltier I felt about seeing Andrew, the more obligated I felt to Peter. After all, how could I be upset with Peter over anything when I was doing something so heinous behind his back?*

Halfway through the magazine, her grandmother's clock chimed four o'clock. Peter would be home in a couple of hours. No time to start any major undertakings. Magic was sleeping in a neat circle on Laura's stomach while Samantha lounged in a nearby puddle of sunshine. Laura started reading another article in the magazine.

About six thirty, a tremendously loud noise shook the silent house. Peter was unlocking the back door. Magic and Samantha bolted through the house to investigate. Laura, who had fallen asleep, awoke with a start. Before she could shake off her drowsiness, Peter was walking loudly across the polished hardwood floors toward where she lay in a heap in the chair.

"Sure am surprised to see you home so early," he said, taking off his Ray Ban sunglasses to look down at her from Olympian heights with his deep, gentle brown eyes.

"Well, I . . . ," Laura began as she struggled to sit upright in the plump chair.

"It looks like you've been there all afternoon," said Peter, smiling at her. When he smiled, his entire face crinkled up in an appealing expression that served him well in sales. He was handsome in a classic way, Laura thought: tall, square-jawed and square-shouldered, thick dark brown hair neatly parted on one side, his skin smooth and boyishly ruddy. He wore great-fitting, conservative suits, one hundred percent cotton shirts and pure silk ties. But despite his traditional uniform, a look vital to a salesman's success in right-leaning Cincinnati, Peter often enjoyed wearing some little flamboyant item. Today it was a red cord holding his Jack Nicholson style sunglasses around his neck. Some days it would be a tweed touring cap or red suspenders.

"Peter, I have to tell you something."

To Peter, she looked so small and kitten-like in the over-stuffed chair that he knelt down in his business suit and hugged her. She was warm and soft to the touch, like a cat in a sunbeam.

"You won't want to hug me when you hear what I did today," she murmured in his ear as he held her.

Peter's arms stiffened as thoughts of the evil Andrew engulfed him.

"I quit my job in Elaine's new business. I am totally, completely unemployed. We left it open so that I could someday go back, but I'd be too embarrassed to ever do that."

Relieved that she had no Andrew-related confessions to make, Peter hugged her even harder. "Good for you. I know it wasn't working out very well. I saw even less of you in your new job than in your old one."

"You're not angry?"

"Of course not."

"What about our pledge that neither of us would make any major career moves without consulting the other?"

"Well, it's okay," Peter said, stopping himself just before plunging off the precipice by adding, "since you're a woman."

"I feel so weird. I haven't been unemployed since I was fifteen. I worked during college and every summer break. I even worked for temporary services during Christmas and spring breaks."

"It's okay, sweetheart."

"And here I wasted a whole afternoon reading and sleeping. I should have used this time to do something useful around the house. I've been absolutely worthless."

"It's okay to be worthless for a day," said Peter as he held her tighter. For some unknown reason, he found the thought of Laura waiting for him, curled up in the big chair, appealing. It was a comforting mental image, like his mother's leaving his bedroom untouched while he was away at college. Now he had another secret, safe place where he could shed his armor and lie naked on the bed.

□

The next morning, Thursday, dawned a perfect spring day. Peter and Laura sat as they did every morning at their round oak kitchen table reading the *Cincinnati Enquirer,* but today Laura still wore her bathrobe and shearling slippers.

"Honey, could you pass me the Metro section?" Peter asked as he folded the sports page. As he glimpsed at Laura across from him, her ruffled white cotton nightgown peeking from beneath her plaid robe, he smiled.

"Here it is," Laura said, passing Peter the section he wanted. "I'm really going to start pounding the pavement today. I'll have another job lined up before next week."

"Well, don't rush. Don't settle for just anything. You don't want to get yourself in another intolerable situation."

"You're a fine one to tell me what to do. I can't think of a more stressful job than printing sales. You get it from both ends, the plant and the customer. So don't lecture me about avoiding stress. Just rest assured there's no danger of my becoming a *haus frau*."

"You don't want any bon bons, then?"

"Absolutely not."

Peter returned to the Metro section, but Laura, unable to focus her mind on current events, studied his thick, gold wedding ring as his strong hand curled around his coffee cup. *I got so tired of sneaking around, trying to hide my relationship with Andrew from Peter and everyone else,* she thought. *I remember how relieved I felt when I finally told someone about it. Too bad the person I told was Elaine. She was my best friend at Northwest, but she was no help at all. She said, 'follow your heart.' But I didn't know where my heart wanted to go.*

Laura began rummaging among her painful but fascinating memories of those days. After about ten months of the excruciating predicament, the inevitable happened. Andrew, who at first had claimed to be content with stolen moments together, lost patience. One Sunday afternoon he drove to Peter and Laura's house. They were sitting on their front porch drinking iced red zinger tea and playing Scrabble. This is when the yelling and hammer-wielding incident had occurred. That episode shocked Laura into determination to end the adulterous relationship.

After Andrew drove off that day, Peter demanded that she tell him about everything, even the sex. *That was the worst part. My guilt felt like an actual physical pain in my chest. I'd never considered myself the kind of person who would commit adultery. I still can't believe I did it. And here I am, eating breakfast with a wonderful, loving husband and everything seems so cozy. Two cats in the yard and the whole bit. But I know who I really am, and I never thought I would be that kind of person.*

Chapter 3

This Old House

□ ■ □

A week later, Laura had been absorbed into the neighborhood daytime routine. On one unseasonably warm spring day, she went grocery shopping in the morning and found the local store as different in the daytime as her house. Gone were the tired, stopped-by-on-the-way-home-from-work people in their suits or work uniforms. Instead, the aisles were full of slow moving older people and women wading along with many small children in tow.

Laura had worn khaki walking shorts and a peach colored polo shirt. An older woman struck up a conversation about a new brand of coffee cakes that had suddenly appeared on the shelves. Laura found herself seriously discussing whether it was worth taking a risk on the new product just because it was on sale, or sticking with the old favorite. In another aisle, an ancient woman guided an ancient man who clung to the grocery cart as they bickered over every selection. In the last aisle, Laura held her breath as she selected yogurt while standing next to an extremely obese woman with a vile odor.

When Laura approached the checkout area, she noted that instead of several lanes being open, as was usually the case when she shopped after work, only one lane, commandeered by a chatty middle-aged grocery clerk, was available. *Perhaps the store management thinks we daytime people have plenty of time on our hands, so it doesn't matter if we have to wait in line. They think we aren't like the important, busy, working people,* thought Laura as she waited in the long line. *But then maybe I'm the only person here under eighty who doesn't have a job. Maybe everyone else works night shift.*

She entertained herself by squinting to read the outrageous headlines in the newspaper tabloids: "80 Year Old Woman Gives Birth to Mermaid Twins" (why did such publications' stories often describe weird feats of reproduction?) and "Computer Found in Ancient Ruins" (an abacus, no doubt). Then she began overhearing a nasty conversation behind her.

"I'm going to smack the piss out of you."

"Gah!"

"Justin, put that down. I'm going to beat your face."

"Suffasuffaju"

"You little brat, stop that."

Laura heard a smacking sound and turned around in time to see a thin-faced young mother, her belly bulging with a future victim, slapping a baby who sat in the front seat of a cart overflowing with groceries. Amazingly, the little boy, who wore a faded Mickey Mouse T-shirt, did not cry, as though such interaction with his mother were the normal course of events. He continued gurgling and cooing in what Laura considered a charming fashion as he pointed up at some paper flowers that were twisting slowly from the ceiling. His face was grimy and his blond hair uncombed, but his huge blue eyes gazed eagerly at everything.

Not wanting to stare, Laura turned back toward the nearing checkout counter, but no longer found the tabloids amusing.

"Justin, leave that alone. You stupid kid, do I have to slap you all the time?"

"Geesadorf."

As she heard more slapping, Laura cringed. Her mind raced to compose a stinging remark for the horrible young woman: *Are you too ignorant to realize that child can't talk or understand what you're saying? Don't you know that his behavior is simply one of awe at the brave new world he finds himself in? You are probably permanently damaging his young psyche with your constant belittling remarks and threats of physical violence.*

Suddenly, it was Laura's turn to unload her groceries onto the conveyor belt. She was careful to arrange the heavy items first so they wouldn't crush the fragile ones as the clerk pushed them down the chute to the lanky, disinterested bag boy. Laura was busy making sure the scanner recorded the prices correctly and writing out her check, so she said nothing to the tyrannical, young Madonna. She suspected the woman would not be receptive to her comments anyway.

But the image of the abusive, angry mother with the beautiful but unkempt child would not leave her. This vision would haunt Laura during many fitful nights to come as she cried silently to God, *Why are such people fruitful, while I am barren?*

Laura knew the modern term for their condition was "infertility," or "difficulty in achieving pregnancy" as her doctor put it. (Why was everything in her life something that had to be "achieved"?) But in her heart, Laura knew the only expression that adequately described her state was the stark King James epitaph: barren.

Laura was fascinated by her daytime forays into the Price Hill neighborhood around their stately older home. She discovered the reality of what she had always known intellectually, that many of their neighbors were very poor. Laura often thought she must be the only person at the store who bought groceries with real money. Everyone else seemed to use food stamps. Compared with their work associates and friends, she had always felt that she and Peter lived rather modestly. But in her own neighborhood she felt conspicuously wealthy.

They had purchased their house with the same optimistic zeal that makes people enter the stock market. Similar

Cincinnati neighborhoods had seen their majestic older homes invaded by yuppies. But these neighborhoods were mostly on the east side of town. She and Peter had been shocked at how comparatively cheap real estate was on the west side. They reasoned that since it was just as close to the heart of the city and the interstate system as the popular east side neighborhoods, Price Hill was bound to increase dramatically in value someday, too.

For years Laura had endured J. D.'s bragging about how little he paid for his first house in East Walnut Hills, one of the gentrified east side neighborhoods, and how much he sold it for a few years later. Each time he told the story the figures grew wilder. At first, he had bought the house for $30,000 and sold it for $70,000. By the time Laura resigned, he had bought it for $18,000 and sold it for $110,000. Still, despite his exaggerations, Cincinnatians did love their older neighborhoods and impressive profits were possible.

But having lived in Price Hill for three years, Laura and Peter were finding their neighborhood particularly obstinate to increases in property value. A hundred years ago, the neighborhood had been filled with hardworking, often prosperous immigrants—Polish, German and Italian—and still boasted several gorgeous Roman Catholic churches with their attendant elementary schools. But most of the immigrants' children and grandchildren had moved to neat tract houses in the suburbs. Much of the local real estate was owned by absentee landlords and elderly folk left behind.

The other, newer constituency in the neighborhood was Appalachian people who had come to the city in search of employment. Laura was accustomed to being called a "Price Hill Hillbilly" by her friends, and she would always indignantly rebuke them for their offensive attempt at humor.

The problem with Price Hill was that neither the elderly immigrants nor the struggling Appalachian newcomers could afford to maintain their aging homes. One could buy or rent a mansion in Price Hill for a pittance, but one needed a fortune to restore these once magnificent older homes to anything like their former grandeur. Except for pockets of bargain-hunting young urban professionals, the average Price Hill resident could barely cover the rent or mortgage. So the people of Price Hill lived in houses with glass doorknobs, hardwood floors and stained glass windows which were slowly, sadly peeling and crumbling and decaying into the ground.

While Laura and Peter would hire competent professionals to repair the roof or paint the trim, their neighbors performed home repairs themselves, using the cheapest materials. The result of their labors always dismayed Peter, who would wonder, "Why would they buy such a gorgeous house if they weren't going to fix it up properly?"

As Laura carried groceries from her car into her kitchen, her mind still reeling from the ugly vision of the young mother in the grocery store, the phone began ringing.

"Hello?"

"May I speak to Laura Morton?" a young female voice asked politely.

"This is she speaking."

"This is the personnel office at Our Lady of Mercy Hospital. We have received your resume in response to our ad for a public relations assistant. Are you interested in interviewing for this position?"

"I believe so." Laura was scrambling for a pen and something to write on while her chocolate chip mint ice cream melted on the kitchen counter.

"Mrs. Hogarth would like to interview you tomorrow at ten o'clock. Do you know where we're located?"

Laura had sent out so many resumes she couldn't remember which public relations position she had applied for, or even why she would do such a thing. She had answered ads for any position even remotely connected to her bachelor's degree in English.

"I think so, but perhaps you'd better give me some directions anyway."

Laura wrote down the directions, hung up and hurriedly finished putting away the wilting groceries. To her horror, she found that she enjoyed organizing the cans in the pantry and the boxes in the freezer. The sun streamed through the kitchen's white eyelet curtains, bouncing off Laura's blue willow dishes as they rested behind the leaded glass doors of her kitchen cabinets.

Her chore completed, Laura wandered into the living room to check the mail. It hadn't come yet. Somewhere a lawn mower droned, wearily signaling the beginning of another grass cutting season. The spring day was warming up. She went to the dining room and turned on the central air conditioning at the thermostat box. Then she turned it off, deciding she shouldn't waste energy on herself when she wasn't working. Besides, with its high ceilings and deep front porch, their house didn't become unbearably hot on warm days until late afternoon, when the sun slanted at a killer angle through the west windows.

Deciding that cleaning the bathroom would be a suitable penance for an unemployed person, she headed for the bathroom. Until she landed another job, Laura had laid Beulah off.

Scouring powder in hand, Laura turned on the water in their venerable pedestal sink. She was greeted by an insolent belch followed by a stream of brownish fluid, then nothing at all.

□

That night she met Peter at the door with coupons for a local fast-food restaurant.

"The plumbing went out again. The problem is just in our house. I called Mrs. Luebbers next door and Mrs. Busmeyer across the street and their water's fine. Hoffmeyer plumbing will be out tomorrow."

"Oh, wonderful. More money down the drain, literally.

Wait a minute. You talked to our neighbors? You know any
of them?"

"Since I've been off work, I've talked to some of the older
ladies a couple of times. They're very nice. By the way, I
had a job interview scheduled for tomorrow, but I had to
cancel it."

"Couldn't you work the plumbers around your interview?"

"You know how plumbers are. It's hard enough to get
them to tell you what day they're coming, let alone what
time. And I had to beg and tell them it's an emergency."

"I just hate for you to miss a career opportunity. It's not
fair. I tell you what. I'll stay home tomorrow—I'll call in to
work and explain."

"I don't mind. You've got that Procter and Gamble job in
the works and you don't want to blow that account. I can
handle it. Besides, the job was in public relations at a
hospital and that doesn't sound like what I want. I might
be able to use my writing skills on news releases and
promotional mailings, but the rest of the job would be the
pits."

"Whatever you want to do is fine. I appreciate your
taking care of this old house."

"Some days it's almost a full-time job. It's like the house
doesn't want me to go back to work."

"Crafty old thing. Hey, I'm not in the mood for burger
heaven. Let's go someplace decent."

"You could talk me into that," Laura laughed.

Upstairs, Laura shuffled the dresses in her closet,
trying to decide what to wear to dinner. Dressing up had
become a special activity since she'd been out of work. As
she stroked one of her favorites, a red silk dress with black
soutache trim, Laura remembered wearing it to a small
restaurant that overlooked the city the night she told
Andrew she wanted to stop seeing him. *This dress would
have been more appropriate for starting an affair than ending one,* she thought, *but I told Peter I was going to the
symphony with Elaine and had to wear something ap-*

*propriate for Music Hall. Sneaking around like that was so
teenagery. How could I have ever let myself get mixed up in
anything like that?*

Ending the affair had been messy. Andrew was furious.
He accused Laura of using him. There were late night
telephone calls, including one vehement exchange between
Peter and Andrew.

Even though Northwest was a company of some three
hundred employees and their jobs no longer required them
to work together, Laura couldn't completely erase Andrew
from her life. Sometimes she passed him in the hallways,
or he called her extension or cornered her in an elevator or
the research library. Each time he spoke to Laura, his message was the same: he was worried about her, he still
cared about her, he just wanted to talk to her. This subtle
harassment continued for nearly two years, until Laura
left Northwest to work for Elaine.

*Peter was so understanding after he found out about
Andrew, it was unbelievable,* Laura thought as she slipped
the red dress over her head. *When he admitted that his behavior was part of the problem, I felt more in love with him
than ever. In an odd way, I think the affair almost helped.
our marriage because it forced us to be honest with each
other.*

Eventually, the wounds had healed; and even though
the scar remained, Laura and Peter started talking about
having children. The end of the affair was like a cancer
going into remission. The remission caused rejoicing, but
the disease's toll dampened the happiness.

Chapter 4

The Wasteland

□ ■ □

"Guess what, honey. We're not pregnant."

"I really thought this might be the month."

"I think that every month. Well, sorry to bother you at work. I just wanted to let you know since I was a little late this time."

"I really had my hopes up."

"So did I. As usual, I got tired of waiting for nature to take its course and bought one of those little pregnancy test kits at the drug store."

"I guess those things are accurate."

"It says here in the directions that 'this test proved ninety-eight percent accurate in detecting pregnancy when performed by a test group of two hundred females not trained in laboratory procedures.' So that's pretty certain. This kit has two little yellow beads that go in the solution. If you're pregnant, one of the beads is supposed to turn blue within fifteen minutes, while the other bead stays yellow to use for comparison. Mine's been in there over half an hour, and the little marble thing is still as yellow as can be."

"That's different from the last test you used."

"There's an infinite variety of these kits. Some are supposed to form a ring in the bottom of a tube, some have little sticks that turn pink. If I had saved all the money I've

spent on drug store pregnancy tests we could send a kid to
college."

"Don't worry about it. It's worth it to know for sure so
you don't have to spend every minute of the day wondering whether or not you're pregnant."

"That little marble thing is just like my tiny little world.
It's like I'm all wrapped up in this one problem, and
there's no room in my life for anything else."

"I know what you mean. Sometimes I feel like we eat,
breathe and sleep pregnancy."

"I know. I'll let you go. Tonight we're having chicken in
lemon pepper sauce."

"Sounds great."

As Laura hung up the kitchen phone, she felt a wild
urge to call her mother. She dialed the first three digits,
then changed her mind and hung up. She started to empty
the dishwasher, then sat back down on the kitchen stool,
leaned over the counter and dialed her mother's number
again.

"Hi, Mom. How's everything going?"

"Laura! What a surprise."

"I just thought I'd call and see how you are. I just found
out I'm not pregnant—again."

"I knew you never should have taken the pill for all
those years."

"But Mom, lots of people take the pill and still have
babies."

"It's just that it allows women to postpone having
children until past their most fertile years."

"Lots of women my age have their first babies." Laura
wondered why she ever felt the desire to call her mother.
It must be the same instinct that makes a person want to
look over the edge of a high balcony.

"Well, we're worried about your grandmother. We took
her for tests yesterday."

"Could they figure out what's wrong?"

"No, and I think her doctor is purposely dragging his

feet because he thinks she's old and going to die soon and
it doesn't matter."

"Grandma being ninety-six years old doesn't mean she's
going to die soon. Look how many other times the doctors
have given up on her and she's pulled through."

"Anyway, as always, she can't understand why they
can't give her something to instantly make her feel better."

"While I'm between jobs, I've been wanting to spend
more time with her. Would you care if I came over this
afternoon?"

"Of course not. We hardly ever see you."

"I'll be over in about an hour."

Seeing Grandma was exactly what she needed, Laura
decided, even if it meant visiting her mother's house to do
so. For the last three years, her grandmother had been
living with her mother, like a thriving African violet in a
room full of dead philodendron.

As Laura drove to her parents' home in the suburbs, she
thought of earlier trips to visit her grandmother in Toledo.
Grandma had lived in an enormous Tudor style house
with two staircases, leaded French glass doors leading into
the dining room, and a living room so large that a baby
grand piano fit unobtrusively in one corner.

During her childhood, Laura's parents had owned a
series of large, older homes in various tree-lined parts of
Cincinnati. But when her father took early retirement five
years ago, they bought their dream home—a plain-looking
ranch house with only a couple of stick-like saplings in the
front yard. To them, however, this was a smart, modern
home. They couldn't fathom why Peter and Laura chose to
live in a dilapidated old house, just as they couldn't understand why Laura and Peter cherished their hand-me-down
oak bedroom set. Surely a young working couple could afford some new furniture. Laura's parents had started
housekeeping with that old bed and dresser but put it in
the attic as soon as they could afford new plastic laminate
Danish modern furniture in the sixties.

Laura pulled into her parents' flawlessly blacktopped driveway, walked up to the front door and rang the bell.

"Sweetheart, you don't have to ring the doorbell. This is your home." Her mother always greeted her with that statement.

"No, it's not, mother. You never just walk into our house without ringing the bell. I just want to treat you with respect."

"Hmmpf," snorted Laura's mother absently, less concerned about winning the time-worn argument than in shaming Laura for becoming an adult.

"How's Grandma?"

"She's in the living room trying to read the paper, as usual. Why don't you go in and visit while I fix us a snack."

Laura wandered into the living room, where her grandmother sat in a wheelchair next to a pole lamp. She was holding a newspaper about six inches from her face and squinting through thick eyeglasses.

"Hi, Grandma!"

"Why, it's Laura! Come here and hug your old grandma."

Laura bent down and wrapped her arms around her grandmother's shrunken body. Laura remembered when her grandmother's hugs were ample and vigorous. This was like embracing a ghost.

"Grandma, how are you?"

"I'm just fine, except for my eyes. I can't see right nomore and they won't do anything a-tall for me. Some days I see all right, but some days I can't make out nothing. I think I need new glasses."

Had Laura's mother been there, she would have reminded Grandma that the eye doctor said the condition was due to hardening of the blood vessels in the eyes and nothing could be done. Then Grandma would have said, "But I've never had this before." Then Laura's mother would have replied, "But you've never been ninety-six years old before."

Laura just smiled and said, "I sure hope they can do

something. Oh, I brought over some old photos I thought
you might be able to help me figure out, if it won't bother
your eyes. They're some you gave me when you moved out
of your house."

Laura pulled a worn manila envelope from her purse. It
contained ancient black and white photos, and although
Laura could identify each person, horse and farm house
from years of poring over them with Grandma, she knew
her grandmother enjoyed seeing them. Besides, the photos
often lead to interesting stories about relatives long dead
and ways of life long forgotten.

The people in the photos wore stern expressions, as
though peeved at being dragged out of their envelope
again for modern day scrutiny.

"Here's my half-brother, Charles, right after he moved
to Toledo. He never was happy in West Virginia. That was
some suit he wore."

"Where was this photo taken, Grandma?"

"That? That's our old farm house in West Virginia near
Morgantown, afore we moved to Toledo. See, there's my
husband, Clyde, oh, he's been dead some forty years now."

"Who are the little children?"

"Those are my children. Let's see . . . that's Earl and
Anna and Gilbert, Opal, Lucy, and your mother, Mildred,
my baby. Wasn't she the teeniest thing?"

"How did you make it with six children?"

"It weren't easy then. People didn't make big money like
they do now. Clyde wanted to move to Toledo to find work,
so we did. I don't know how we done it. But families loved
each other then. There wasn't all this fussing and fighting
like you see on the television nowadays."

Laura stifled the observation that old-fashioned family
stability was an illusion created by women's previous
economic dependence on men and lack of reliable birth control. In most cases, women had no option but to stay with
their husbands, no matter how miserable the marriage.

Laura looked closely at the small photo she'd seen a
thousand times. As she studied the six solemn children ar-

ranged like stairsteps on either side of her grandmother
and grandfather, she noticed something new. Even in her
loose, waistless farm dress, her grandmother looked stran-
gely plump in that photo.

"Grandma, in that picture you look pregnant. Were you?
Did you lose a baby after you had Mom?" Since she and
her grandmother often talked of dear relatives and friends
who had died—this was one of Grandma's favorite topics—
Laura wondered why her grandmother had never mentioned a lost child if one existed.

"No, no, that's just something on the picture makes me
look that way. You don't think I would let them take my
picture if I was, do you? Women back then wasn't wild like
they are now. Now they parade around no matter how big
they get. Back then we hid such things." Then followed a
cherished story about how angry she was when Clyde
spread the news of the advent of their first child all over
the county as soon as she told him, several months into
the pregnancy. She was only seventeen years old, and even
though she'd been married over a year she was too embarrassed to appear in public after everyone knew she was expecting.

Still, Laura thought her grandmother looked pregnant
in the photo, despite her grandmother's unsatisfying explanation. Perhaps she had lost the child and the memory
was so painful she had completely repressed it. Although
her grandmother was a strong woman who had buried
many loved ones, and seemed to find talking about these
experiences cathartic, perhaps the death of this baby had
been unusually traumatic.

Laura's mother entered the living room with a tray full
of Oreos, Diet Coke and hot tea for Grandma.

"We were just looking at some old photos," said Laura.

"Oh, I've seen all of them a thousand times," said
Laura's mother as she stirred a little sugar into
Grandma's tea. "Mom, let me know if you have to go. You
haven't gone since lunch."

These references to intimate activities, which Laura's

mother made as casually as she would discuss the
weather, did not seem to offend Grandma's sense of dig-
nity; but they always disturbed Laura. Laura reminded
herself that she did not have to care for her grandmother
the way her mother did, and therefore had no right to
criticize.

"Look at this photo of Grandma and all you kids in front
of your house in West Virginia."

"Yes, I've seen the picture, but I can't remember that
house. We were all so small then. Your aunt Opal is the
oldest, and she was only nine."

"I was telling Grandma how she looks pregnant in this
picture."

"It's probably just the dresses they used to wear. They
were like big, loose sacks. Look at those long sleeves. Can
you believe they worked in the fields on hot summer days
in those long sleeved dresses? I guess they had to be loose
so they could move around since they didn't have knits
back then. The only time a woman had a waistline was
when she wore an apron."

"People didn't used to run around almost nekkid like
they do today," observed Grandma.

"Speaking of your Aunt Opal, Laura, would you mind
dropping some things off at her house on the way home?
You drive right by there and I hoped you wouldn't mind."

"Sure, Mom."

□

Walking up the cracked steps of the sixty-year-old apartment building where Aunt Opal lived, Laura remembered
how she had worried during her teenage years that she
would end up like Aunt Opal. Opal was a spinster who
could have sprung from the pages of an English murder
mystery. She had been a "career girl," working as a
secretary at the water works until she retired. She was
tall and thin and had excellent posture. She was cold na-
tured and wore shawls or cardigans, even in the summer.
Laura always thought aunt Opal could have posed for the

Old Maid on the children's playing cards. As a teenager, Laura had considered spinsterhood the cruelest hand life could deal.

"Hello, Aunt Opal. Mom wanted me to drop this bag of stuff off for you."

"Well, Laura! Come in, come in. I haven't seen you in ages. How's your grandmother?"

"She seemed fine to me. Still complaining about her eyes, though. Her vision must not be too bad, however, since we looked at old photos most of the afternoon and she could pick out every detail."

"Well, her vision comes and goes. Our family always was one for having a lot of photos taken, for back then. We never had any money, but photos were always important to Mom and Dad, for some reason. Could you identify them all?"

Laura knew Aunt Opal enjoyed looking at old photos as much as Grandma did. Noting that it was only four o'clock, and Peter would be working late that night, Laura pulled the folded manila envelope from her purse.

"Now, this one puzzles me. It's a picture of you kids and Grandma and Grandpa in front of your house in West Virginia, taken not long before you moved to Toledo. To me, Grandma looks pregnant in that photo, but she denies it."

"Let me see that," said Opal, frowning as Laura handed her the picture.

"I thought maybe she lost a baby and the experience was so painful that she had repressed it and couldn't remember it. Something like that would be horrible."

"Well, she lost a baby, all right."

"Was it a boy or a girl? Did it die at birth or live a little while?"

"It was a baby girl, but she was born very sick. I'm sorry, Laura, I can't give you any more details," said Opal, her lips pursed.

"But it happened so long ago, I'm surprised that Grandma can't remember any of the details. She can remember what kind of horse she used to ride to church when she was a girl, even though she usually can't remember what she did yesterday."

"Maybe she can remember it, but just doesn't want to talk about it."

"Oh."

"Some things are better left unsaid. I've said too much already. If you don't want to hurt your grandmother's feelings, please don't ever let her know I told you as much as I did."

"Oh, I won't."

Opal handed the photo back to Laura as though it were a secret map to the cursed tomb of a pharaoh. Laura looked at the photo again. Her grandmother's dress was definitely bulging under her stiffly folded arms. Who was that child, gone so long ago, who no one wanted to remember?

O Day of Rest and Gladness

□ ■ □

Sunday morning dawned bright but misty. A cool, sweet smelling breeze made the peach colored priscilla curtains in Laura and Peter's bedroom dance. Magic and Samantha were stretched out on the window sill of the room's bay window, their bellies pressed against the screen. Laura woke up before the alarm, feeling like she was in a perfume ad.

She turned over and hugged Peter, whose broad back and shoulders faced her. He rolled over and began stroking her shoulder, though his eyes were still closed. Laura smiled. He was such a good man, showing affection even when he was unconscious. Laura's eyes traced his familiar face with delight. After seven years of marriage, she was intimately acquainted with every mole and tiny bump. Not that there were many imperfections in Peter's strong face with its prominent features under impeccably combed dark brown hair. He was a large man, teddy-bear like but a few pounds short of being fat.

"What time is it?" he mumbled, eyes still closed.

Laura squinted at the digital clock. "Seven-thirty."

"Hmmm. . . , we have over an hour before we have to get

up for church," Peter noted, opening his eyes and smiling gently at her.

"Well, not exactly. Remember, this is my first day teaching Sunday school. I've got to be there by nine o'clock, so I really ought to get up now if I'm going to have time to shower and eat breakfast."

"So much for our one day to sleep in a little."

"Peter, I thought you were behind me on this. This is something I feel like I really need to do."

"I just hate to see anything eat into the little bit of time we have together."

"Please be supportive today. I'm nervous enough as it is. Let's don't fight."

"Fine. I'm going to get a little more sleep. Wake me up when you're done with your shower." Peter stretched and rolled over, turning his back to Laura. "Why do I always have to be supportive of everything that takes you away from me?" he mumbled.

Ignoring his remark, Laura hopped out of bed and briskly put on her robe. *Why does Peter always consent to anything I want to do, but balk when the time comes to follow through?* She wondered as she entered the old-fashioned circular shower curtain in their immense claw foot tub.

□

Laura wandered into the junior high Sunday school classroom, hugging the teachers' guide to her chest. She had carefully read the lesson, looked up all the Bible passages, underlined the key concepts and made notes in the margins; but somehow she sensed that this hadn't been adequate preparation.

Their church was rather small, and Laura was relieved to see that only five young human beings sat around the classroom's long table.

"I'm terribly sorry I'm late," she said as she slid into a seat at one end of the table and began anxiously arranging her papers. "My husband and I were eating breakfast, and time got away from us, this being our only day to sleep in and all." She realized she was rambling. None of the students, who were much too large to be children, but certainly didn't look like adults, were paying any attention.

The three females were sitting with their heads huddled together, whispering and laughing furtively.

The two boys were sitting—sort of—in chairs as far away from the girls as possible. One of them had removed his shoes, a fact Laura decided to ignore. They were laughing and guffawing loudly, but Laura couldn't understand a word they were saying.

"Hi! My name is Laura, and I'm your new teacher. I'm really looking forward to getting to know all of you."

Maybe two of the girls were listening.

"Let's turn in our books to page twenty-four and just jump right in. This is a really exciting lesson, all about the prophet Amos in the Old Testament. He was just a simple sheep herder, but God called him to preach to the people of Israel about . . ."

"Laura!"

"Yes, and your name is . . . "

"I'm Kristen. Can I be secretary today?"

"Secretary?"

"Yeah, fill out the attendance book and count up the money and take it down to Mrs. Roll's office."

"Well, I guess so. Here's the attendance book and the offering envelope." In her eagerness to impart great spiritual truths, Laura had forgotten these chores.

"No fair. Kristen did it last week. Let somebody else have a turn," interjected an outraged girl with dark curly hair.

"Okay," said Laura. "Who hasn't done it in a long time?"

All three girls raised their hands. Meanwhile, the two boys continued to snicker in some alien tongue.

"Why don't one of you boys be our secretary today?" Laura suggested innocently. The boys began to hiss and chortle like a mad scientist's assistant.

"You can't let the boys do it!" said the curly-haired, preteen girl.

"Why not?" asked Laura.

"They'll just mess it up."

"Oh, I'm sure they can do just as good a job as the girls. Right guys? Now, which of you wants to be our secretary today?"

After some snickering and staring at the floor, the boy who had removed his shoes picked one of them up and tossed it across the room. "Ain't going to be no secretary," he muttered, his first intelligible words of the morning.

"I'm sure you can do a fine job," said Laura, not realizing that she was placing his budding manhood in serious jeopardy by handing him the secretary's book. His male companion snorted in glee. But the unwilling secretary was a formidable opponent, and suddenly his eyes twinkled with a splendid idea. After a few months' experience, Laura would have recognized this particularly dangerous facial expression, but since this was her first day she naively handed him the book and envelope. Only when she glanced at the record book the following week would Laura discover that the girls had been given names such as "Froog" and "Spacehead" and that heavy metal rock groups had also been recorded as "present."

□

After the Sunday school hour, Laura rushed to the church vestibule where she was supposed to meet Peter. He was late, and they slipped in just before the choir's processional.

"I almost gave up on you!" whispered Laura as they settled into a back pew.

"Why didn't you?" asked Peter sullenly.

"Aren't you going to ask me how it went?" asked Laura.

"I figure I'll hear all about it."

They rose as the chords of the first hymn began, "O Day of Rest and Gladness."

□

"I just can't believe how tired I am after teaching only

five kids for one hour. How do their teachers handle a
whole roomful of them for six hours a day?" Laura was
giving Peter all the details of her morning as she vigorous-
ly tore the lettuce for their Sunday dinner salads. "I really
feel like I failed. I don't think they heard a word I said.
Kids today aren't like we were when we were in Sunday
school."

"How do you mean?" asked Peter as he checked the
turkey slices cooking in the microwave.

"We weren't angels, but we had a little respect for our
teachers, even if we didn't like them. We had at least a little interest in spiritual things. These kids just want to gos-
sip and make jokes to put each other down. They didn't
listen to the lesson. They didn't ask or answer questions.
They giggled while I was trying to lead a closing prayer."

"Going to quit?"

"No. Absolutely not. I've been feeling for a long time like
I need to do more in the church. We don't do any more for
God than our friends who don't even claim to believe in
him."

"But we're so busy. We have almost no free time
together as it is. I'm all for going to church, but let the
housewives and old ladies worry about it. We don't even
have any kids of our own in the Sunday school program.
It's just not our responsibility."

Laura was slicing cucumbers fiercely. "I am a housewife,
Pete," she said, her eyes glistening.

"No, you're just between jobs. But if you want to be a
housewife, I'm all for it. Do whatever you want to do. I just
want you to be happy. Just make up your mind and do it.
Whatever you decide is fine with me. I'll be supportive. I'll
be good." Peter was slamming plates and silverware down
on the round oak table in the breakfast nook.

"But I want to know what you want, too. I want to consider your feelings when I make my decisions!"

"Why? So you can do just the opposite?" Peter muttered
as he placed folded cloth napkins under the forks.

"That's not fair. I do care about what you want. I just

don't know what I want. I'm in limbo. I don't want to
charge full steam ahead into my career when I'm trying to
get pregnant. Actually, what I really want is a baby. It
seems like everyone else in the world can have one except
me."

"I'm sorry. I guess I'm a disappointment as a husband
because I can't give you a baby."

"That's not what I'm saying at all. We don't even know
whose fault it is, and anyway it doesn't matter. This is
driving me crazy but I can't even mention it around you
without your interpreting it as some kind of personal attack on your masculinity."

"Well, it's hard to watch your wife pining away for a
baby and know it's probably your fault."

"Peter, why can't we talk about this like mature adults
without hurting each other's feelings? Anyway, it's probably my fault. I'm the one with irregular cycles."

"Let's just drop it. We're both hungry and cross. The
turkey's ready."

Peter and Laura consumed Sunday dinner in silence in
their cheerful kitchen with the yellow walls and eyelet curtains. Peter read the Sunday sports page while Laura
leafed through a catalog as they ate.

□

Later that same Sunday afternoon, Laura baked a fresh
apple cake, one of her specialties. Peter heard her banging
around in the kitchen and roused himself from sleeping on
the couch with the Sunday *Enquirer* folded on his
stomach. He switched off the basketball game that was
blaring unwatched on the television and wandered
towards the delightful aroma.

"Smells great, sweetheart."

"I'm baking this for the fellowship pitch-in tonight. But
they always have so many desserts that I guarantee
there'll be some left over."

"Oh, I forgot about fellowship. Do you think we could

skip it this time? I'm really beat. I feel like I need this day to get rested up for the week. It's going to be a rough one."

"Fellowship is only once a month. There's a missionary speaker afterwards who's supposed to be really interesting."

"Maybe you could go without me, although I was looking forward to spending some time with you."

"Good grief, Peter. We have college friends on the mission field this very minute. Your friend Nick is a full-time youth pastor in the inner city. It's not like we're sacrificing our all for Christ to go to one pitch-in dinner."

"Sorry. I forgot how unworthy I am."

"I didn't mean that. I just don't think it's unreasonable to ask you to go to this dinner with me."

"That's fine for you. You can sleep all tomorrow morning if you want to. I have to call on Henry Thompson in the morning. The weekends just go too fast."

"Well, I'm sorry. I forgot that I'm a lazy and unimportant person."

"You know that's not fair. I just don't understand why you have to be so involved in the church all of a sudden."

"We're not very involved in our church at all. We don't go to Wednesday night Bible study. I'm not in the women's circle and you're not in the men's group. You know, we are actually very marginal members."

"Marginal members who almost never miss a Sunday and always keep their pledge paid up? All churches should have such marginal members. And now that you're teaching Sunday school, we'll never get another Sunday off."

"A Sunday off? It's not like going to church is a job that you deserve a vacation from!"

"Laura, being a Christian doesn't mean you have to be there every time the church door opens."

"'I was glad when they said unto me, let us go to the house of the Lord. . . .'"

"You know what I mean. Jesus never said, 'You have to be at church constantly or you'll burn in hell.' In fact, I remember him saying something about man not being created for the Sabbath, but the Sabbath for man."

"The Sabbath must be created for man with all the hours of sports on television on Sundays."

Peter rolled his eyes. "Laura, all I'm saying is that I just don't understand why we can't miss this one pitch-in."

"I'm just trying to be a good Christian. Sometimes I think maybe God has made me barren to punish me for not being committed enough."

"Don't use that word 'barren.' It's self-pitying and stupid."

"It's how I feel. If that's stupid, I'm sorry."

"Well I don't know why you can use dramatic words like 'barren,' but if I try to communicate how I feel about our not getting pregnant you make sarcastic remarks."

"When did I ever do that?"

"I don't know, I didn't write it down. You just tell me I'm not secure in my masculinity or something neat like that."

"Peter, why are we fighting?"

"I don't know. All I wanted to do was to enjoy Sunday afternoon. But I guess that isn't holy enough around here."

"Please, let's don't fight. I can't take any more stress."

"Neither can I." With that, Peter returned to the couch and the newspaper and the NBA.

Chapter 6

The Cosmic Chuckle

□ ■ □

A month later, Laura was in Liberty, Indiana, standing in the food line at Peter's family's annual Memorial Day picnic, preparing to ignore all guidelines for sensible eating.

"Did you hear Caroline's big news?" said Peter's mother, who had been flitting through the crowd.

"No, what?" asked Laura.

"Oh, I thought she would have told you by now. I'd hate to take away her fun in giving you the news—why don't you ask her?" And with that Peter's mother, a plump, jolly woman with droopy eyes, slid away to greet an aunt and uncle who had just arrived.

Laura continued filling her plate with baked beans, grilled hamburger, potato salad and slaw. She then made her way to a folding chair by Peter's sister Caroline and her husband, Roger.

"What's this I hear about good news?"

Caroline's round face flushed with a mixture of joy and pain under her glossy, short brown hair. "We're expecting a baby in November. We just found out last week."

"That's wonderful. I bet you two are excited," Laura replied evenly.

"We sure are. I can't wait to find out if it's a boy or a girl," said Roger, pushing a hot dog into his mouth.

Caroline looked somber. "I know you and Peter have been trying for some time. How's it going?"

"My doctor gave me a temperature chart when I went for my last checkup. I'm supposed to record my temperature every morning for three months and then make another appointment, but I xeroxed it and think I'll keep it for six months before going back. I'm still not really worried because my parents also had trouble conceiving, and they eventually had four kids."

"Oh, I'm sure everything will work out well for you two," said Caroline enthusiastically.

"Anyway, I'm very happy for you both. By the way, how are those business management classes you were taking?" Thus Laura deftly steered the conversation away from the dreaded topic of fertility.

□

That night Laura and Peter lay in bed "spooning," as Peter called it, with Peter lying on his side in a semi-fetal position and Laura's body cupped against his back.

"Peter, it's just not fair."

"What's not fair?" he answered sleepily.

"Caroline's being pregnant."

"Well, they've been married three years. It's not exactly shocking news."

"I mean, she's four years younger than you, yet she gets to have the first grandchild in your family."

"I know. I'm not thrilled about that. I guess I always thought I'd produce the first grandkid, being the oldest and all. But it's really not that important."

"I guess not."

"Let's just be happy for her and Roger."

"Well, there's the other reason it's not fair."

"What do you mean?"

"You know."

"No, I don't know. What do you mean?"

"The abortion."

"I never should have told you about that. I wasn't even supposed to know myself—I found out by accident. Anyway, that was seven years ago. You know that guy she was going with was a creep, and she was just a kid. I think abortion is wrong, too, but if ever there was a case for it, it was Caroline."

"Still, she threw away a perfectly good baby. And now she's pregnant. I thought I was unworthy of motherhood, but I've never . . . done that."

"Honey, it's late. You're not being rational. I wish you'd get off this punishment kick. Poor Caroline deserves some happiness. What's done is done."

"Intellectually, I know you're right, Peter. I love Caroline. She's a dear friend. And I know that whether or not Caroline gets pregnant has nothing to do with us. But emotionally I can't help feeling jealous. It's so hard to be happy for her even though I know I have no right to be upset."

"Just remember that her pregnancy and we are not connected. It's not like there are only so many babies to go around and her being pregnant means we won't get one."

"You're right, sweetheart. I'm being ridiculous."

"I know you can't help the way you feel, but you'll do us both a big favor if you don't become obsessive about it."

"Now you sound like everybody who tells us to relax, like it's all our fault for not relaxing. Relax. Relax. If one more person tells me that I'm going to spit on them."

"You don't sound very relaxed," Peter chuckled.

"This isn't funny! How can you joke about it?"

"I'm not really joking. I'm just trying to cope."

Laura began to cry softly, too quietly for Peter to hear, though he could feel her body gently heaving. He ignored it for a moment, then rolled over and hugged her close to him.

"It's all right, honey. Please don't cry. It makes me feel so bad when you cry about this."

"I know, Peter, but I just can't help it." Laura was sobbing audibly now. "I don't want to be rational tonight."

"Well, be irrational just this once. Say whatever you think, and cry as much as you want, and don't worry about it."

"It's not fair. It's not fair at all."

Peter held her tighter.

"She's four years younger than me. She's only been married three years and we've been married seven. She's even had an abortion. If I'm not good enough to be a mother, why is she?"

"Just let all your bad feelings out, Laura."

"You should have the first grandchild; you're the oldest. Why is she the lucky one? Why can everybody in the world have a baby except me?"

Peter stroked her while she shook, his own tears flowing silently into her hair.

□

The next morning, Laura was up early. She fixed Peter his favorite breakfast, French toast, and plopped down across the table from him, cradling a cup of cappuccino in her hands.

"I'm really sorry about last night."

"That's okay. Sometimes a person has to let go, to lose control a little."

"Yeah, but I lost control a lot. You know I didn't mean any of the nasty things I said about your sister. I really love Caroline. She's a great person."

"I know you didn't mean anything, honey."

"Her being pregnant has nothing to do with us. I'm really and truly very happy for her."

"I know you are," Peter said as he leaned across the table and rubbed the side of her face. Laura looked at him, thankful for the touch. Peter sat back in his chair, smiling at her, not realizing he had dragged his favorite silk foulard tie through the syrup.

"By the way, do you need me to pick up anything for our dinner with Nancy and Michael tonight?"

"No, I've got everything I need. I thought I'd fix the chicken in mushroom sauce, salad, rolls and strawberry shortcake."

"Sounds great. I've got to run. See you tonight."

Peter threw on his suit jacket, stuffed some papers in his briefcase and kissed Laura fleetingly on the mouth as he glided out the back door.

Laura sat at the kitchen table for a few minutes after he left, listening to his car on the gravel in the driveway and kids yelling at each other on the way to school. Inside, she could hear her grandmother's clock ticking loudly on the mantel.

Samantha slunk into the room, hopped on Laura's lap and began fluffing her bathrobe and purring in ecstasy. "You're about as useless as I am," Laura told the enraptured feline. "Your mommy's got to get busy," she said as she shoveled the reluctant cat off her lap. She wanted to clean the house thoroughly for their dinner guests. She'd have no time to send out resumes or call phone numbers in the want ads today.

□

Nancy and Michael lived in Mt. Lookout, another neighborhood of venerable older homes on the more fashionable east side of the city.

"Did you have any trouble finding us?" Peter asked as he took their coats.

"No, I've traveled to the west side a few times and had a general idea where Price Hill is, and you gave excellent directions," Nancy replied, smoothing her glen plaid pants over her ample figure and straightening the bow on her red silk blouse.

"I hope you didn't have any trouble passing through customs," Peter grinned.

"No, we just brandished our passports and they waved

us through," answered Michael as the two couples settled
into the overstuffed furniture in the living room.

"I've never seen a town so divided into east and west sections like Cincinnati," said Laura, entering the living room
with a tray of hors d'oeuvres.

"I guess it's the natural layout of the city, with
downtown and the interstates bisecting it," observed
Michael, looking serious in his tortoise shell rimmed glasses and button down shirt. Peter had met Michael, who
was an architect, while playing racquetball a few months
earlier. The two couples had gone out together a few times,
but this was the first time Michael and Nancy had been in
Peter and Laura's home.

"There's more to it than that," said Peter. "The west side
is more blue collar, more provincial."

"Yes, westsiders do tend to ignore the other parts of
town," said Michael.

"No more than eastsiders," said Laura. "You know, the
last time I was in the gift shop at the art museum I saw a
poster that was a cartoon style map of Cincinnati showing
all the historic and cultural sites. It showed downtown and
several east side neighborhoods like Walnut Hills, Mt.
Adams and Hyde Park, but not one single west side neighborhood, even though they're just as old and historic. The
map ended before it got to the west side—it just cut it off."

"Well, let's not argue about the merits of east versus
west," laughed Nancy. "That's been done to death in this
town. Your home is as beautiful as any on the east side. I
think it's just a matter of time until Price Hill gets discovered. Laura, tell us how everything is going with your
job hunt."

"Just fine," Laura answered, cringing inside. "I'm taking
my time looking this time. I know I'm being too picky, but
I want to find a place where I can put down roots and stay
a long time. But, Nancy, your work is so interesting. How's
everything in the world of social work?"

"No great crises, for the time being. Oh, big news for one
of my clients. You know I've told you about Rosalie?"

"Yes, isn't she the one who's working as a clean up person at a bakery?"

"That's her. She's doing great and her success will hopefully help me place other clients in competitive employment. But the big news is that she's pregnant. She's due in December."

"You're kidding. I didn't know mentally retarded people were allowed to get pregnant," said Peter.

"Well, they're not prisoners," responded Nancy. "They have the same rights we have."

"I know that," said Peter, annoyed at appearing bigoted. "I just mean that having a baby is a big responsibility. Is she married? How is she going to support the baby on a cleaning person's paycheck? I mean, anyone who is having a child has to answer those kinds of questions."

"In our world, yes. But not everyone thinks like us," said Nancy. "Rosie isn't married, and after talking it over with the father they've decided not to get married. He works in one of the county's sheltered workshops. I'm going to be her labor coach and go to her childbirth classes with her. We're ironing out all the details."

"This is a really naive and stupid question," said Laura, "But won't the baby be mentally retarded, too?"

"No, both Rosie and the father became mentally retarded during childhood—Rosie had Reye's syndrome and the father had a bad reaction to a DPT shot—so there's no reason why they should be any more likely to have a baby with mental retardation than anyone else."

"But how will she raise a child? How can she teach it things?" asked Laura.

"She'll need a lot of help, that's true. But they'll make it. People do. One of the social workers in my office has a client who lives in your neighborhood who has nine children. I don't know how she does it, but she survives."

"Honey, maybe we could talk about something besides your work and your clients for awhile," said Michael, smiling wryly at his wife.

"I'm sorry. I never seem able to leave it at the office," said Nancy, blushing under her flawless makeup.

"No, it's very interesting," said Laura, as she filed away one more argument to hurl at God in the night. Now people with mental retardation living in poverty are having babies while she, well educated, healthy, prepared, was denied access to the coterie of motherhood.

□

"Well, this has been a great week," said Laura at breakfast. Peter, hurrying to finish his coffee, looked up from his newspaper.

"In what way?" he asked.

"You don't know?"

"Would I ask if I knew?" he replied as sweetly as he could.

"So far, I've found out that two other people are pregnant—one of them is younger than me and one of them is mentally retarded. Not to mention all the girls I see pushing strollers in the neighborhood who look like they are about twelve."

"I'm worried about you, Laura. You are becoming bitter over this. We can't start evaluating every other person's right to have a child. We're not the judge of everyone's moral fitness for parenthood. Maybe you should go for counseling or something."

"Bitter? Oh, now I'm bitter. I need therapy. Sweetheart, it's something I've dreamed about all my life, and I'm bitter because I'm disappointed that it isn't happening to us. I'm supposed to be happy for all these other people who get pregnant, never mind that I want to be pregnant, too, but might never be."

Peter put down his coffee and folded the newspaper. He went over to Laura and put his arms around her as she hunched over in her chair. "Sweetheart, you're being unreasonable. We haven't even begun the infertility treatment course. They can do so many things these days. Maybe one of us has a little medical problem, or we might need our hormones fine tuned. And even if we never do have a baby, we've got each other, and that's more than most people ever have."

"You're absolutely right," said Laura. "But I don't think I need therapy. It's just been a bad week. I swear, if I find out one more person is pregnant I'll completely lose it."

"I've got to go, sweetheart. Are you sure you'll be all right?"

"I'm fine. Have a good day. Why don't you call me at noon?"

"I'll try if I don't end up having to take the client from Nashville to lunch. I'll be glad when his company's job is off the press and he leaves town. He's about the most irritating person I've ever met, and we've had to entertain him all week."

"Well, I guess I'll just see you tonight." Laura smiled and kissed Peter as he bent down on his way out the door. She heard him walk to the garage, turn on the ignition and pull out of the driveway. The clock ticked in the living room. The secret daytime life of the house was beginning.

Suddenly, the phone rang loudly in the quiet house and Laura shuffled to answer it.

"Hello?"

"Laura?"

"Yes?"

"This is Pat. I've been thinking about you a lot lately. How would you like to get together for lunch sometime this week?"

"Great! When?"

"Anytime. What about today?"

"Sounds good. Where do you want to meet?"

"Why don't we eat at the Red Squirrel on Fifth Street downtown? They have the best doubledeckers and are fast, too."

"That sounds good. At twelve o'clock?"

"I'll be there. Take care."

"Bye."

This is wonderful, Laura thought. About eleven o'clock

that morning she began putting on her favorite navy blue
linen suit. Pat, a lawyer in a downtown office, would be ex-
quisitely attired and Laura didn't want to look like the
dowdy housewife friend, even if they were just going to a
sandwich shop. Laura was dismayed to find that the suit's
skirt, which had always been somewhat loose, was fitting
snugly. *I thought I'd been eating more since I've been at
home. I know I've been making more home cooked meals.*
How long had it been since she'd worn that skirt? Almost
two months? It didn't seem possible.

She picked out a red and white polka dot blouse with a
red and white striped bow tie, but found she had trouble
tying the bow—one end kept coming out shorter than the
other. *To think I used to dress like this every day,* Laura
thought as she slipped her stockinged feet into her navy
blue pumps. Recently her wardrobe had consisted of
shorts and blue jeans and Reeboks. She had even done the
unthinkable once and worn a sweat suit in public.

As Laura skillfully guided her Honda through the heavy
traffic, she felt alive and purposeful. Downtown always
made her feel that way. Maybe after lunch, she'd linger a
while and do some shopping. Though their finances were
tighter since she was not working, they were in no great
danger. Nevertheless, the loss of Laura's income meant
she had to curtail non-budgeted purchases. And what fun
was shopping if she found something she liked but
couldn't buy? Maybe she'd go to the public library on
Ninth Street instead. With its huge central atrium open to
massive skylights far above and plants hanging over the
banisters on each floor, the library was a good place to
recharge the soul and a cheap place to sit and read and
think.

Pat was waiting at a table in the Red Squirrel, a tiny
sandwich shop tucked away on the downtown skywalk.
She wore a plum suit with a lavender blouse and an interesting print scarf tied expertly in an asymmetrical tri-
angle. Her short black hair curled under perfectly. She
was looking through horn rimmed glasses at some papers

from her wine colored leather briefcase. *She looks like
she's the star of one of those very-serious-about-business
computer commercials,* thought Laura. *I can't believe she's
the same person I knew in college who wore blue jeans the
entire four years.*

"Pat, it's been ages! How's everything going?"

"Oh, great, and you?" Pat removed her glasses and
stuffed her papers back into her briefcase.

"Well, it didn't work out for me at Elaine's new business.
Our personalities didn't mesh in that kind of work environ-
ment. Right now I'm taking a little time off to look for a
job I can really pour myself into. But that's boring. What's
new with you?"

"Things are going great at the firm, more work than
ever. And Tom's still in heavy equipment sales and enjoy-
ing it. But we've got some good news and some, well, not
bad news, but some not so great news."

"Let's hear the good news first."

A young blond waitress came for their orders. Pat ordered ham and swiss cheese on rye, while Laura opted for
the diet plate.

"We're building a house in Villa Hills."

"In Kentucky? That's a gorgeous neighborhood. When
will it be finished?"

"Oh, in December, about a month after our baby is born."

"Baby?"

"That's the not so great news. I've always wanted
children some day, and since I'm thirty-two my old biological clock is ticking away. But this isn't a great time. We
make this great financial leap and are building our absolute dream home, and this happens. They know better
than to blatantly discriminate against me at the firm over
this, but they can do subtle things to sabotage my career.
They just don't trust pregnant women, even though I tell
them I'll work just as many hours after the baby's born as
before. I've already been passed over for some of the good
cases and I think my pregnancy was the main reason. And

they almost never give any women of child bearing age any key litigation. But at least Tom is happy about it."

"This is so ironic," said Laura, staring at her water glass.

"Why?"

"We've been trying to conceive for fourteen months with no success, and you get pregnant accidentally. You were probably even using birth control."

"We always do. But I was having cramps and it was time for my period, so just that once we didn't. I don't see how I could possibly have conceived. But don't be discouraged. Fourteen months isn't that long. My sister and her husband have been trying for four years."

"Have they had any luck?"

"Well, no, but they haven't had all the available tests and treatments yet. Sandra says they won't give up until they do. They've spent about three thousand dollars of their own money so far, and their insurance won't cover most of the medical expenses. But her doctor is still optimistic since they've ruled out some of the most serious and irreversible causes of infertility."

"You know, you're the third person I've found out is pregnant this week. It's really weird. It's like some cosmic force is trying to rub my nose in it."

"I'm sorry; I didn't mean to make you feel bad. I know where you're coming from. Sandra says it seems like everyone else in the entire world is pregnant but her. Everywhere she goes, she says, she sees nothing but fat, pregnant women."

"Don't be sorry. I'm happy for you, Pat. And don't worry, everything will work out for you somehow. Things always do."

"I know everything will work out for you, too. Now, let's talk about something besides babies, babies, babies, or we'll both get depressed."

□

After lunch, Laura decided to go straight home. Her feet

were tired in the unaccustomed pumps. The sky looked
overcast and she had no umbrella.

As she walked in her back door, the phone began ringing. She raced to pick it up before the answering machine
clicked on.

"Hi! This is me."

"Oh, hello, Peter. How's your day going?"

"Just fine. I called at noon but you weren't in."

"I met Pat for lunch downtown. You won't believe this,
but she's pregnant and doesn't want to be because they're
building a house in Villa Hills. Doesn't that figure? Three
people—this week I've found out three people are pregnant. It's too much to be coincidence."

"Are you okay, Laura? Do you need me to come home?"

"Don't worry about me. I'm not coming unglued. It's just
so ironic. It's been a rough week, but I still have plenty of
hope."

"So do I, honey. Well, I've got to run. Just wanted to
make sure you were all right."

"See you tonight, sweetheart. We're having lasagna."

"Great. Goodbye."

After Laura hung up the phone, she pulled off her
pumps and undid the button on her skirt. The gray sky
finally began delivering the storm it had been promising
all day. Lightening flashed and a mighty thunderclap
roared outside. The rain made the inside of the house a
silent, private world. Halfway across the living room,
Laura felt an uncontrollable urge to kneel down at the
flowered Queen Anne sofa. *Oh Lord*, she prayed, *please forgive my selfishness and pettiness. Please give us a child,
too, and we will teach it your ways, oh Lord. Amen.*

She stood up in the darkened room, feeling awkward
even though she was alone. *Well, it worked for Samuel's
mother, what was her name? Hannah, I think. Of course,
she promised to give up her baby as soon as he was
weaned. I couldn't do that. But then, if I had a baby and
took it to our church and left it there, our preacher would
have me arrested. But that's not the point. Maybe I'm not*

*as sincere or dedicated or committed as Hannah was.
Maybe I don't have the right reasons for wanting a child.
But then, other people don't have to analyze their motives
to death. They just get pregnant without even thinking
about it.*

   She walked up the staircase, pausing at the large oval
window on the landing to look out at the rain beating
down on the empty yards and streets outside.

A Relative Ordeal

□ ■ □

Later that rainy afternoon the mail plopped loudly through the mail slot. Magic ran for the front door and stood proudly on top of the letters that had fallen on the floor as though they were a prize kill. Laura, who had been reorganizing her closet upstairs with Samantha's help, came downstairs to investigate the commotion. This dramatic daily routine was a highlight of her days since she had been at home.

Two bills. *Peter won't like these. I'd better put them in the bill box before he gets home. No sense ruining his day.* Three letters from people wanting money for important causes—the Lung Association, the American Bible Society and World Vision. *I'll put them in the pile. She read the message printed on the outside of an official looking envelope. A two thousand dollar line of credit has been preapproved and is just waiting for us. How nice. I'll pitch that. But what's this?*

Laura examined the fragrant, peach colored envelope with an unfamiliar address embossed on the back flap: Mrs. Naomi J. Rosenberger, 303 East Third Street, Cleves, Ohio, a nearby small town. Inside was a single sheet of

matching peach stationery that was covered with a tall,
graceful, looping handwriting.

Dear Laura,
We have never met, but Opal told me about you and gave
me your address. Opal is the only one of my brothers and
sisters who knows about me. She told me you were asking a
lot of questions the other day, and I thought that since you
are my niece you deserve to know who I am. You would
probably find me sooner or later since I live so close.
There are some family secrets that you don't know about
and perhaps shouldn't know about. Please do not mention
this letter to your mother or any of her brothers or sisters. I
trust you will keep my confidence.
Sincerely,
Naomi Rosenberger, your aunt

Outside, the thunderstorm had turned into a gentle
rain. Laura pulled the thick Cincinnati telephone book off
the massive library table in the den. It would be too easy if
the newfound aunt were listed. Rosenbergs, then Rosen-
bergers. N J Rosenberger, Clvs . . . 555-4763.

Laura wrote the number on the note pad by the phone.
She arranged the pencils in the carved pencil holder and
straightened the bills in the matching carved bill box,
checking the due date on each one to make sure none were
past due. None were. Next she dug the stray rubber bands
out of the small cut glass dish they used to hold paper
clips and put them in the library table's small drawer.
Finally, she dialed the number.

A loud, old fashioned ring seemed to echo in a large
space. In her mind, Laura could see a white farm house
with dark woodwork and faded lavender wallpaper. She
let the phone ring six times and was about to hang up
when a thin, female voice said, "Hello?"

"Hello. This is Laura Morton. Aunt Naomi? I got your
letter today . . ."

"Well, I didn't expect you to call. I thought you might write . . ."

"I hope I'm not imposing, but I'd really like to meet you. Could I come visit you sometime?"

"Do you work?"

"No, I'm between jobs right now."

"Well, how about next Monday at noon? I'll fix a little lunch." Naomi did not sound surprised by Laura's phone call.

"Oh, that would be wonderful. I'm looking forward to it."

"Let me give you directions to my house. Have you ever been to Cleves?"

"No."

"Well, you get on River Road . . . "

After she hung up, Laura sat listening to the rain and wondering about Aunt Naomi. Laura had time to think these days. Often fifteen minutes would pass before she'd realize that she hadn't done anything but sit and stare. When she worked in an office, she used every precious second to accomplish something. Those days contained no unaccounted for moments. She would have thought it boring to sit still for five minutes, let alone fifteen minutes. Laura realized she was not the same person who used to leave the house every morning at 7:30 a.m. to drive the 12.5 miles to Northwest Press.

□

The day of the visit to Aunt Naomi was a chilly, rainy Monday. That morning Laura could concentrate on nothing more taxing than looking through her old photos again and again. Finally it was time to leave.

Aunt Naomi had given good directions, and Laura found her house easily. It was not the lumbering clapboard farmhouse she had pictured, however, but a trim little brick Cape Cod with a neat front yard and two white dormers. She walked up the steps and rang the doorbell, feeling like an adult Nancy Drew.

Aunt Naomi answered Laura's timid buzz quickly, open-

ing the door with a solemn face. They did not embrace.
Naomi resembled Laura's Aunt Opal, tall and lean but
more fragile looking. Her face was folded into a few firm
wrinkles and she wore glasses with cat-eye shaped lenses
like the ones Laura had worn as a child in the 1960s.

"Well, you must be Laura. I don't know if you have
much family resemblance. The only one I've seen is Opal
and you don't look like her, except for being thin."

"You look very much like Grandma in some of the old
photos she gave me. I brought some of them along in case
you'd like to see them." Laura fumbled in her purse for the
worn manila envelope. "Here's the one that made me think
you might exist. Grandma looks pregnant in this photo,
but she and everyone but Aunt Opal denied it. Grandma
seemed to feel a lot of anguish when I questioned her
about it. I thought maybe you had died at birth and she
was repressing a horrible memory."

"As far as she's concerned, I did die at birth," said
Naomi. She lead Laura through the immaculate little
house, which was filled with plastic laminate furniture
and loud orange plaids that must have been stylish in
some past decade, to the kitchen, which looked like the set
from an old black and white sitcom. Lunch was waiting on
a small formica topped table: tuna fish sandwiches cut
into quarters on melamine plates with potato straws on
the side.

"I have so many questions, Aunt Naomi."

"And I have so few answers," the older woman replied.

"I don't want to pry. But I'm terribly curious about what
happened and why no one in the family knows about you.
I'm so glad to get to meet you. I love all my aunts and am
thrilled to have another one," Laura said, aware that she
was babbling.

"Well, it's a simple story, really," said Naomi, pouring
two tall glasses of iced tea. "I was a depression baby. Your
grandmother gave birth to me in West Virginia just before
they went to Toledo. I was apparently a very sick baby,

and your grandmother left me with a local doctor who offered to take care of me."

Following Naomi's lead, Laura bowed her head for a quick, silent prayer. "Buy why didn't they go back to get you later, after you got well?"

"That's what I've been wondering for the last fifty some years," Aunt Naomi answered grimly. "I suppose I shouldn't complain. The doctor's family—their name was Gilbert—treated me like one of their own, although they never formally adopted me. No one was rich in those days, but compared to other folks we were fairly well-to-do. Dr. Gilbert, whom I consider my father, passed away in the fifties of a heart attack. He was a great man, well loved and respected in the community. We lived in Philippi, West Virginia."

Laura hurried to swallow a bite of tuna fish as her aunt paused. "Why didn't you keep in touch with your other brothers and sisters? Why all the secrecy?"

"I don't know. That must have been your grandmother's idea. You wouldn't believe how women kept their pregnancies hidden in those days. But Opal was old enough to realize that I had been born. She looked me up several years ago. I made her promise to keep my existence a secret. I guess that after all those years, I didn't have the energy or the desire to meet the rest of my natural family. I had plenty of family through the Gilberts and my in-laws."

"Well, how did you end up in Cleves, Ohio?"

"Oh, that." Naomi smiled for the first time since Laura's arrival. "I married the most wonderful man, Frank Rosenberger, in 1950, and we lived in Belington, West Virginia. He was a doctor, just like my father. He had family in Cincinnati, so when his health forced him to retire in 1975, we moved here. He couldn't bear to actually live in the city— he despised big cities—so we found this little community not too far away. But he passed away five years ago, and life hasn't been the same since."

"I'm sorry. I would've liked to have met him," said

Laura, munching on the potato straws. She didn't know
they still made them.

"Laura, have you told anyone about our little get
together today?"

"No, not even Aunt Opal. I wanted to talk to you first."

"Good. You didn't even tell your mother?"

"I don't tell her much at all. We don't get along the best.
I mean, we love each other, but she is very critical and a
take-charge type of person, which can be useful sometimes. But if I'd told her, she might have tried to come
along and handle everything. I didn't know what your
story was and didn't want to cause any trouble or hard
feelings in the family."

"Thank you. Despite my reservations, I'm glad I got to
meet you, Laura. But please promise you won't tell the
rest of the family. I just don't feel up to meeting everyone
and trying to start relationships with all of them. My life
is complete as it is. I don't have enough energy for that."

"I'll do whatever you ask. But I know they would love to
meet you. It would be such a wonderful surprise to discover they have a sister they never even knew."

"That's the problem. They never knew me. We don't
share any childhood memories. The family that raised me
had two little girls of their own. They're my sisters."

"But maybe you would find a bond that goes deeper
than memories if you were reunited with your family?"

"I cannot be reunited with those people because I never
was united with them in the first place. Your grandmother
gave me away at birth. I never spent a day living under
the same roof with your family. Now, are you going to keep
my secret?"

"I will keep this to myself. But I wish you would reconsider seeing my grandmother. Grandma was so upset
when I asked her about her being pregnant with you. I
know she would love to know what happened to you, to see
you. You are her child. She carried you inside of her.
Would you please let me arrange a meeting with her? I
know she wouldn't tell her other children if you didn't

want her to. I just know it would mean a lot to Grandma if
you would see her. She's ninety-six years old and not in
very good health."

"Laura, you're young and you're romanticizing the situation. What your grandmother did was the same thing as if
she had an abortion. She didn't want me then, I don't see
why she would want me now. I consider Mrs. Gilbert my
real mother."

"Did you ever have any children, Aunt Naomi?"

"No, Frank and I were never able to conceive. That's
probably my greatest regret in life."

"My husband, Peter, and I have been trying to conceive
for well over a year now, and I'm starting to despair, so I
know how you feel."

"The doctors can do so many wonderful things these
days to help people like us." Aunt Naomi's expression sof-
tened and she smiled at Laura. "Don't give up hope."

"I'm a long way from giving up hope at this point," said
Laura, who hadn't meant to talk about herself. "But I am
trying to be realistic and prepare myself for the worst."

"Well, that's a mature attitude, but a sad one," said
Naomi. "You know, I have enjoyed getting to meet you. I
had thought it would be an ordeal. Maybe some day I will
contact some of my other blood relatives. But I'm just not
ready now."

"Please reconsider visiting Grandma. She may not have
much time left—at ninety-six you never know. I know she
must have had a good reason for whatever happened, and
she would want to see you."

"No, that I don't think I can do. We can't change history,
Laura. What's done is done."

"Do you mind if I keep in touch?"

"Of course not."

"When is your birthday, Aunt Naomi?"

"July 23. Why do you ask?"

"I want to be sure to remember you on your birthday,
like I do my other aunts," said Laura, who was the sort of

person who could support an entire Hallmark franchise by herself.

"I like you, Laura. I wish I could've known you all your life. But that's just another thing my biological mother deprived me of. I know it may not sound nice, but I am being honest. That's why I don't think I can ever meet her. I feel too much bitterness."

"Well, I'd better be going," said Laura. "If you change your mind, please let me know." For once, she knew she would have more to tell Peter when he got home than he would have to tell her.

"Goodbye, dear," said Naomi, awkwardly finding Laura's hand and squeezing it.

Chapter 8

The Institute of Fertility

□ ■ □

The next day, Tuesday, dawned as clear and bright as the previous day had been overcast and gloomy. Laura walked Peter to the back door that morning to kiss him goodbye. She stood on their small back porch for several moments after he had gone just to enjoy the lush greenery of their overgrown backyard in the early summer. Unkempt honeysuckle spilled over the graying wooden privacy fence while tall, ancient oak trees towered overhead.

Feeling full of purpose, Laura went inside and roamed the house like one of their cats as she tried to decide what project would most benefit from her unexpected energy. She couldn't understand why she felt so enthusiastic and optimistic, since she had left her Aunt Naomi's house heavy-hearted the day before. But today was one of those days that burst at the seams with boundless potential.

Laura strolled through the house, up the stairs to her bedroom and began getting dressed. As she did so, her eyes were drawn to the small, nearly empty bedroom next to theirs. She seldom entered this room, and usually kept the door closed. But for some reason, probably feline related, it was open today (none of the door latches in the old house worked very well, and the cats had learned that with a little prodding most of them would swing open).

Laura entered the tiny room, which they used to store unpacked boxes and odds and ends they hadn't found a place for since they moved into the house.

The sun streamed through the room's two large windows onto three small cardboard boxes stacked one on top of the other. These were filled with copies of *The Horizon*, the campus newspaper Laura had written for in college. In one corner, a hideous black lamp with a faded pink ruffled shade perched atop a rickety end table. Both were family castoffs she could never bring herself to give away. The lamp's black, squat ceramic base looked like a leftover prop from the Arabian nights, perhaps home to some uncooperative genie. In another corner, a conglomeration of curtain rods and venetian blinds stood sloppily at attention.

Laura tried to picture the room's lilac wallpaper, now darkened with age, replaced by a sunny yellow pattern and its drab green woodwork painted white, as she planned to do when this room became a nursery.

Samantha was spread out on one of the wide window sills, basking in the sunlight. Laura scooped her up and held her baby-style, an action not particularly to Sammy's liking. Laura sat on the cardboard boxes containing the old newspapers and began to talk to the annoyed beast.

"See, here's where we'll put the baby crib. And the changing table goes there. We'll have a big rag rug in the middle of the room and a rocking chair. That's where I'll rock my baby, you silly cat. You'll be my little cat baby until then, won't you?" Sammy yawned. She was a complacent animal and had resigned herself to enduring Laura's affections. "My sweet little cat baby," crooned Laura.

Suddenly, she decided what to do with this perfect day. She set Samantha down with some gentle pats. Sammy stretched and ambled back to the window sill from which she had been so rudely hoisted.

I've been moping and waiting for lightening to strike and not doing what I can do about this situation, Laura told herself as she strode down the stairs and into the den. *Maybe God wants me to put feet to my prayers.* This thought was a reference to a sermon illustration she had heard years ago. The story had struck her as stupid but had, for some unknown reason, stuck in her head like an irritating commercial jingle.

In the story, two women hoped for years that God would remove an unruly brothel from their small town. Each night the more sanctimonious of the two women said a long prayer to that effect, while the other woman listened. One morning the faithful prayer warrior awoke to the good news that the brothel had burned down during the night. As she was rejoicing, she told her unpretentious friend, "I knew the Lord would answer my prayers." The friend held up an empty gasoline can and said, "So did I, but I put feet to my prayers."

Laura pulled open the top drawer of their old metal filing cabinet and began leafing through the files she maintained on every conceivable subject. *Incentive* (pictures of fat and thin women clipped from magazines to put on her refrigerator during her next diet), *Income Taxes* (several very thick files), *Individuals* (clippings from newspapers and magazines about people who might make good characters in a novel some day), *ah, here it is, Infertility.* She pulled this file from the drawer, sat down at the library table and began leafing through it. It contained clippings or Xerox copies of every article she had found in the last year on the subject.

Finally, she found the one she wanted. It was a local newspaper story about a gynecologist who had started a clinic called the Institute of Fertility. Laura liked the positive way it was called the Institute of Fertility instead of the Institute of Infertility. People having difficulty "achieving" pregnancy could go to the clinic to learn about the available options. It offered laser surgery, sterilization reversal, artificial insemination, in vitro fertilization,

gamete intro fallopian transfer, sperm cryopreservation
and could even make arrangements with surrogate
mothers. Laura didn't know what all the words meant but
was encouraged by their solid, scientific sound.

She dialed the clinic number and made an appointment
for later that day for an initial consultation. It was as
simple as that.

She felt a little disloyal going to a doctor other than her
regular gynecologist, Dr. Joan Thomas, but was attracted
by the clinic's anonymity. She could go to the clinic to do
simple research. Her own doctor had suggested a plan of
action and expected Laura to follow through, which she
hadn't done.

After Laura's last examination revealed no obvious
problems, Dr. Thomas had told her to keep a temperature
chart, which Laura had been doing faithfully. Meanwhile,
Peter was to undergo semen analysis, so that if he had a
low sperm count they could correct his problem simul-
taneously. Laura's doctor had said they shouldn't proceed
with any infertility testing or treatment for Laura until
Peter was tested because many of the causes of female infertility were difficult and expensive to detect while most
male problems were easier to pinpoint and remedy.

But Laura was stymied at this point. She enjoyed keeping the temperature chart, even though it was tedious, because she was glad to finally be actually *doing* something
about their problem. Every month they timed their sexual
activity to coincide with the most likely times, at least as
much as this was possible given Laura's irregular cycle.
But she could not bring herself to ask Peter to have the
semen analysis done. Since she was supposed to obtain
those results before she took her temperature charts back
to her doctor for evaluation, she didn't know what to do
next. She knew Peter would gladly agree to the testing,
but she didn't want to risk bruising his masculine pride.
Besides, she didn't know what learning who was responsi-
ble for their infertility would do to the delicate balance of
their marriage.

□

Laura was ten minutes early for her appointment. She couldn't drown a nagging guilt feeling that she should include Peter in this, but she feared that this clinic would also suggest beginning with the dreaded semen analysis. *Besides,* she told herself, *I'm just doing research, planning for a worst case scenario.*

The clinic was located downtown on the fifth floor of an office building. Laura was used to dressing down in the neighborhood and felt underdressed in her navy chinos and windowpane plaid blouse. She signed in at the receptionist's window and took a seat near a magazine rack. Most of the magazines were about parenting, and she avoided looking at the cherubic babies being cuddled on the covers.

After a few minutes, she glanced at the only other occupant of the tiny waiting room, a thin woman with long, stringy blond hair and small, closely set eyes. She was wearing very faded blue jeans, a blue T-shirt and flip flops.

"Hi! I was really surprised they could see me so fast. I just called this morning," said Laura, wanting to start a conversation.

"Yea. They seem real eager to work with you here."

"We live in Price Hill, so downtown is really close for us," said Laura for no particular reason.

"Huh. We live in Price Hill, too, on Grand Avenue near Warsaw. Whereabouts do you all live?"

"On Purcell near Phillips. We're almost neighbors."

"Price Hill is real handy to everywhere. I can hop on the bus and be downtown in ten minutes."

"My husband and I have been trying to get pregnant for fourteen months now, and I thought maybe we ought to do something about it," said Laura. The small woman seemed so sad and kind that Laura found herself blurting out personal information she ordinarily would have been reluctant to tell a doctor.

"I know what you're going through. We done all these ex-

pensive tests and found out my husband needs an operation that costs over $3,000."

"Good grief. A lot of infertility problems are expensive to
solve." The blond woman didn't look like a person who
could find $3,000 easily.

"I already got a daughter from my first marriage, so I
knew everything was okay with me. That's why I want to
be a surrogate mother. They pay all your doctor bills, plus
give you $10,000. We figure I'll have one baby for some-
body else, and then use the money to pay for Harold's
surgery."

"But won't it be hard for you to give up the baby after
you carry it for nine months?"

"It'll be the hardest thing on earth. I'll just keep telling
myself how the baby will make some people who can't
have one so happy, and that'll make it some easier. I don't
know no other way to get $3,000 . . . do you?"

"No, that certainly is a huge sum of money."

A woman in a white lab coat appeared behind the waiting room's tiny sliding glass window. "Hazel Franks?"

"Good luck," the small woman told Laura as she disap-
peared through a white doorway.

Laura sat alone in the waiting room and felt herself becoming sick. The stark pale walls and the garish orange
plastic chairs were giving her a headache, she decided.
She stood up, saw that no one was watching through the
reception window, and slipped quietly out.

*Maybe God doesn't need my feet to answer this prayer.
But that's ridiculous. Fertility counseling is not like arson.
It's not the same thing at all,* Laura thought as she scur-
ried through the well-dressed downtown crowd.

Chapter 9

The Tumult

□ ■ □

That night Peter was watching one of the final games of the NBA championship. It seemed to Laura that the professional basketball playoffs had been going on longer than the regular season, but she managed not to gripe. She had compared notes with her friends on this topic and discovered that Peter was better than most husbands about not letting sporting events dictate the schedule of their lives.

Laura was sitting next to him on the couch, sorting through old counted cross-stitch patterns. She had done a lot of embroidery when she was single and always seemed to have plenty of time on her hands, but it had been years since she'd tackled a needlework project. She had decided to start with a small project, a bib for Caroline's baby, and was looking through cute duckie and teddy bear patterns. *So many women have spent untold hours creating charming masterpieces for infants to drool applesauce on,* she thought with a smile.

The phone rang just as she was counting the stitches in a yellow duck's blue bow. "Could you get that, honey?" asked Peter. The game was apparently at some crucial juncture, so Laura strolled into the den to answer the phone, shutting the door behind her.

"Hello?" Laura answered.

"Laura, this is Sharon."

"Oh my goodness. I haven't heard from you in ages. How is everything?"

"Fine, just fine. I'm still with AT&T. Chuck is doing great at ADP."

"Wonderful. Are you still happy in New Jersey?"

"Oh, yes. But it would be great to see you two again."

"We'll get over there one of these days. You know how Peter is about vacations. He's always too wrapped up in his work to get away for more than a day here and there."

"Actually, Laura, I called you because things really aren't so fine," Sharon said, her voice dropping.

"What's wrong?"

"Well, you know how we've been trying to get pregnant for the past three years?"

"Yes . . . "

"Chuck and I finally conceived."

"Oh, how wonderful . . . "

"But we lost the baby."

"Oh, how awful."

"It was an ectopic pregnancy, you know, the baby implanted in the tube instead of the uterus. Anyway, they had to remove it surgically, and I now have one less ovary than I had before."

"I've known two other women who had that happen, and they both eventually got pregnant again. And a lot of women get pregnant with only one ovary. It only takes one egg and one sperm."

"But we had so much trouble conceiving before, and now it will be even more difficult."

"But at least now you know your system works."

"Do you always look at the bright side of everything?"

"I'm sorry. You must feel terrible. I just don't want you to give up hope. We haven't given up hope yet."

"Well, think how worried you are, and you two have only been trying half as long as we have."

"Oh."

"But I didn't call to compare sob stories. You're one of the few people I can talk to about this."

"I know what you mean. I can't discuss my unpregnancy with just anybody."

"Most people tell you to relax, that you can't get pregnant because you're not relaxed. I can't stand that."

"I know what you mean. If one more person tells us we should adopt a child because everybody who adopts gets pregnant afterwards, I think I'll die."

"Actually, dying doesn't sound all that bad right now," said Sharon. Something in her voice told Laura this was an intentional comment.

"Sharon, don't joke like that."

"I'm not joking. How can God care about me if he lets something like this happen? And if he doesn't care or doesn't exist, what's the point? We've all been deceived."

"Sharon, I know it seems horrible. But after a few days you'll put it in perspective."

"It's been a few days. I was so happy when they told me I was pregnant. I almost couldn't believe it." Sharon's voice was cracking now. "How can a God who claims to love me take away my little baby?"

"Ectopic pregnancies are a medical problem. God didn't cause it any more than he gives someone cancer. It's just a part of living in this world."

"Don't try to preach to me, Laura. You know I've heard as many sermons in my life as you have. They don't change the way I feel."

"Please, Sharon. So many people love you and want you to be happy. All the gang from school—we all care about you. You were the best roommate any college student could ever have. You put up with my all-nighters, my insane nervousness before dates— you're the best. Please promise me you won't do anything to hurt yourself."

Silence.

"Please, Sharon. I love you. Please promise me. I wish you weren't eight hundred miles away so I could come over there and hug you right now."

"I need more than a hug, Laura."

"Please promise me you'll take good care of yourself."

"I can't promise anything, Laura. I'm through being rational. When something irrational happens, it isn't rational to continue to live life rationally. You know what I mean.

"When we were in school, it was all so easy," Sharon continued. "Especially going to a Christian college. My life was so neatly packaged then. I didn't know our God took little babies away from mothers who had prayed for them for over three years. He sends an ample supply of babies to people who live in war zones, in third world countries, to stupid teenagers, but not to me. That's what's not rational."

"Please promise you'll get some kind of help. Maybe you can talk to your pastor," said Laura, her mind frantically praying for the right words.

"Everyone always thinks therapy is the answer. I was a psychology major for two years, remember? Those people don't have any magic answers. They can't change the facts of your life."

"Please, Sharon. I won't be able to rest until you promise me you won't hurt yourself. If you do, you'll be hurting people who love you the same way losing your baby hurt you."

"I know it sounds selfish, Laura, but I just don't care any more. I really shouldn't have burdened you with my depression. I'm sorry I called. Anyway, I'd better get going."

"Please promise me, Sharon."

"Don't worry about me, Laura. I'll be fine. Just don't worry about me. I'll write later. Love ya, bye."

"Wait, don't hang . . . " But Sharon had already hung up.

Frantically, Laura rummaged through the drawer in the library table for her little red address book. Finding it, she dialed Sharon's number with trembling fingers. The line was busy. She waited a minute in horrified silence, then tried the number again. It was still busy.

Feeling numb, Laura walked back to the living room

and sat down on the sofa next to Peter. The basketball game was apparently nearing its exciting conclusion.

"Who was that?" Peter asked, his eyes on the screen.

"It was Sharon."

"That's nice."

"She's had an ectopic pregnancy and had to have an operation that destroyed the baby and one of her ovaries. She's more depressed than I've ever heard anyone, and she even hinted at suicide. I kept pressuring her to promise she wouldn't do anything like that, but I just made her hang up. I said all the wrong things. I shouldn't have pressured her."

"Did you try to call her back?"

"Yes, but she's got the phone off the hook. I keep getting a busy signal."

"Sharon's got a lot of sense. She'll pull through. Don't worry about her."

"I don't know. I never heard her talk like that."

Peter turned off the roaring basketball game, somewhat hesitantly, Laura thought cynically. He pulled Laura close to him.

"Don't worry about Sharon. She'll be fine. She's a very intelligent person."

"These emotions have nothing to do with intelligence. The strange thing is, I really do understand how she feels, although I don't think I could ever commit suicide and hurt the people I love. But I really know how she feels. I think she'll pull through, too, but it's scary. It's really scary. These are such powerful emotions."

"Just keep trying her number throughout the evening. But if you don't get through you don't need to worry. She'll be all right. She just needed someone she could talk to, bare her soul to and all that, like you did the night after you found out Caroline was pregnant. She didn't really mean everything she said. She just needed someone to listen, and you did that."

"Oh, Peter. I handled it all wrong."

"You did your best, sweetheart. I know you did fine."

"Maybe we should pray about this."

"What do you mean?"

"You know, pray about it. On our hands and knees right here and now."

"Oh. Yeah. I know this sounds callous, but do you care if I catch the end of the game? It was tied up in the fourth quarter with only two minutes left. Whoever wins this one goes to the championship. God's not going anywhere."

"Sure. Fine. Let me know when the game's over."

Peter was already turning the television back on. Laura picked up her cross stitch patterns, but had lost all enthusiasm for the project and put them back in the canvas tote bag where they had been for the past seven or eight years. "I'm going to go put these away," she told Peter, who was sitting on the edge of the couch with his chin in his hands, intent on the game.

She walked upstairs and entered the empty future nursery to put the tote bag back in the closet where she stored unfinished craft projects. The room looked even drabber at night. The windows were now dark and floorboards creaked under the cracked linoleum floor as she walked. Laura wondered how long they would have to live with the dismal lilac wallpaper.

Her mind not focusing on any particular thought, Laura sat down cross-legged on the floor. Magic padded softly into the room, her claws scritch-scratching on the floor, and curled up on Laura's lap. Laura began stroking the elegant little creature's soft head as purring filled the room.

Lost in a mournful reverie, Laura didn't hear Peter's heavy footsteps at the door.

"The game's over. The Celtics lost. Not that you care. Thanks for letting me watch it. I'm ready to pray now if you are. How are you doing?"

"I'm fine. I just can't stop thinking about Sharon."

"Do you think you should try to reach her one more time?"

"That's a good idea." Laura stood up and discovered that

one of her legs had fallen asleep. She walked gingerly to their bedroom and found Sharon's number in the small phone directory on their nightstand. Peter went back downstairs. Laura dialed the number, and this time the phone began ringing. Sharon answered.

"Hello?"

"Sharon? This is Laura."

Peter gave Laura the OK sign and left the room.

"Thanks for calling back."

"I hope I wasn't a jerk when I talked to you earlier," Laura began.

"You weren't a jerk, Laura. I was. I had no right to dump on you like I did."

"Are you okay now?"

"No, I'm not okay, but I'll survive. This is the toughest thing I've ever been through."

"I know what you mean. I mean, we haven't been trying as long as you two, but I'm starting to get the idea."

"I know you're going through hell, too. I had no right to make it sound like you couldn't possibly know what I was feeling. Most people have no idea how I feel. I even had one business associate, who supposedly called to cheer me up, remark that I was lucky I didn't lose a real baby. Like just because my baby was almost microscopic he or she wasn't real."

"I know what you mean. Our baby isn't even conceived, but I feel like he or she is a real person. That sounds weird, but every month when I find out I'm not pregnant it's like losing that baby. The pro-abortion people can rationalize all they want. As far as I'm concerned, a baby is a human being from the moment it is conceived. All that is left is for it to grow."

"Sometimes I get so far down that . . . well, it's really bad for me right now since Chuck and I are having problems."

"Oh, Sharon, no. That's all you need."

"This infertility thing is driving us apart. I know challenges are supposed to bring people together, but it isn't

happening in our case. It's like we both feel guilty and
worry about whose fault it is and withdraw into ourselves.
None of the tests have been really conclusive. Chuck's
sperm count is borderline low. He's had it tested more
than once and sometimes it's normal and sometimes not so
good. And my cycles are somewhat irregular, but I am
ovulating. But none of the tests have really told us exactly
what's wrong. They just cost a lot of money and leave us
even more confused."

"I'm just beginning to research our options," said Laura.
"A lot of them are pretty dreadful, and they all seem incredibly expensive."

"Chuck and I have spent over five thousand dollars so
far on infertility tests and treatments. And neither of our
insurance plans cover any of it."

"Good grief. If you have to spend that kind of money you
won't have any left over to raise the child after it's born."

"Finances have caused a lot of our problems. You just
wouldn't believe how much everything out here costs. I'm
still used to midwestern prices. We pay more for our tiny
apartment than most people back home pay for mortgages
on a huge house."

"Seriously, Sharon. I know I was out of line before in
trying to give you advice. I can't even give myself advice.
But maybe you should go for marriage counseling."

"I know. That's what everyone always says when someone has problems. But it's like our problems are too far out
of hand. We both act as though nothing's wrong, but it's
like we're living in some sort of demilitarized zone. I never
know when something will flare up. Then we yell and say
hurtful things and retreat from each other. For some
reason, I feel that going for counseling would be admitting
defeat. It would be the end of the war."

"But you and Chuck have been married longer than we
have. You've always been the perfect couple. I'm sure you'll
work everything out."

"I certainly hope so. I can't explain it and I don't want

you to take sides. I don't want to put all the blame on Chuck. I haven't been easy to live with either."

"Things sure aren't like they were in college, are they?"

"You know, I've been thinking about that a lot lately. I felt so alive and committed and sure of everything then."

"I know what you mean. For a long time, I was sure I wanted to be a preacher or a missionary, and so did Peter."

"Everyone who went to school there did. Let's face it. We had to go to chapel three times a week. It's hard not to think organized religion is the center of life."

"I guess it isn't."

"Not in the real world."

"It's like in a small Christian college all the emphasis is on the spiritual, sometimes at the expense of the real, external world. But now that we're out of college, it's exactly the opposite."

"That's what I like about you, Laura. We never discuss the weather."

"Sorry. There just aren't many people I can talk to about God and religion. Most people think I'm trying to 'save' them or something. People get really scared when anyone discusses anything religious, like it's the supreme embarrassment."

"I know. Even the people in our church are like that. But maybe that's just because this is the east coast."

"No, it's like that here, too. We can talk about our bazaars and chili suppers, but even at church it's hard to talk about faith in God informally. Jesus is usually only discussed during the church service."

"I feel so guilty a lot of the time, Laura. You were raised the same way I was. The church was the center of everything when we were growing up. I feel like I just don't do enough for God anymore. But it takes so much energy just to live."

"I know. I keep thinking how I've got to get back into Bible reading and personal devotions. And Peter and I never have family devotions anymore."

"You once did?"

"When we first got married. It lasted about six months. I feel so guilty about that, but we're always so busy and so tired."

"Chuck and I never even did that much. We meant to but never got around to it. I wish I could recapture that passion I had for being a Christian when I was a teenager. In youth group, at camp, anywhere they had an altar call I was always right there, crying my eyes out. Once I even thought I heard angels singing."

"Maybe you did."

"No, I think it was my youthful imagination. I don't feel excited about anything any more. I guess I'm just too old. You know, maybe that's why I want a baby so much. That's the most exciting thing I can think of happening to a woman."

"I think that's part of the reason I want to have a baby, too. I mean, all my life I looked forward to going to college, to getting married, to having a career. I've done all those things; I'm thirty, and I sometimes feel like life is almost over. Childbirth would be sort of the ultimate life experience, something wonderful to look forward to. But that's an awfully shallow reason for having a baby."

"Now you sound like me," said Sharon with an ironic laugh. "I go over and over in my mind all the reasons I want to have a baby, and I worry that maybe my reasons aren't good enough, that maybe I've got a bad, secret motive, and that's why we're infertile."

"I do the same thing. But then I get mad because other people don't have to go through this. They just get pregnant without all the high anxiety. Sometimes they don't even want to be pregnant. They haven't even thought about it. It just happens to them. This week I've found out that three people I know or know about are pregnant, and it made me feel horribly sad and angry. I know I shouldn't feel that way, but that's how it is."

"I know. It's so unfair. But now that Chuck and I are having problems, maybe it's best that I'm not pregnant. Sometimes I think that having a baby would make all our problems go away, but everyone knows that the absolute worst reason in the world to have a baby is to try to improve a marriage. But I think the problems we've been having are due to the stress of not being able to conceive, of riding an emotional roller coaster every month, with every new test and procedure and prescription. If I got pregnant, I really think our marriage would start to recover. I know we'd still face stresses, but I think preparing for and caring for our child would pull us together. This infertility thing is tearing us apart, pushing us into our own little private worlds of misery."

"Sharon, it's so good to talk to you about these things. It's like having a discussion with myself. You're the only person I've talked to who really understands the way I feel."

"Thanks for calling me back, Laura."

"I couldn't have slept for worrying about you."

"I'll be all right. Really. I'm sorry I dumped all my negative emotions on you. You're just so nice and dumpable. You should have told me off."

"Believe me, I know how low you can get with this problem. I'm glad you called me. It helps me to talk, too."

"Thanks, Laura. I'll call again soon."

"Take care."

"You, too."

□

Laura walked downstairs. She felt relieved that Sharon had sounded, if not happy, at least rational and in control of herself. But the conversation left her pensive.

As she reached the living room, she saw that Peter had fallen asleep on the couch. "Nightline" was blaring on the television; two red-faced, angry gentlemen were trying to insult each other as quickly as possible before Ted Koppel cut them off. Laura turned off the television and kissed Peter on his broad forehead.

"Oh, what, I must have fallen asleep. How's Sharon?"

"She's a lot better. I'll tell you all about it at breakfast. Let's go to bed."

"That's an excellent idea. Laura, um, do you . . . "

"What, Peter?"

"Maybe we could postpone the family devotions to another time when I'm awake."

"Sure. I'm too tired now, too. But I do want us to start doing them again."

"Yeah, I think it's a good idea, too. We've got to get back into that."

Slowly, they walked upstairs together.

Chapter 10

Fertility Is Not Pretty

□ ■ □

The next morning, Friday, Peter was humming at breakfast.

"My but we're cheerful this a.m.," said Laura as she spread conserves on the whole wheat toast. She hadn't brushed her hair yet and was wearing a worn, blue dotted swiss housecoat.

"Today I meet with Simon from New York and hopefully sign the deal for the next four issues of the magazine."

"That would be great."

"This will be the biggest deal I've ever pulled off if it goes through. Not only will the commission be most welcome, but my stock ought to go up around that place."

"I can't wait to find out how it goes. Peter . . . "

"Yes?"

"Don't worry that I'll be a financial drain forever. I really am going to go back to work as soon as I find the right job. I'm just looking for someplace where I can fit in and stay for a few years and build something."

"I know, sweetheart."

"And some day, after I get established in my new job, I want to return the favor for you. You can quit your job and take your time looking around for something really good."

"Don't worry about that. In my line of work I can't afford to lose touch with my contacts. I haven't reached nirvana down there, but things aren't much better at other printing firms. It's a high stress, rush-rush business."

"But I don't want you to resent my being home and having this time to get my act together."

"I don't resent you for that, Laura. In fact, a little part of me actually likes having you here at home. It's kind of neat, something I thought I'd never have."

"That's terrible. How can you say that?"

"Well, let's be honest. It has uncomplicated our lives. You get all the household stuff done during the week so it's freed up our weekends. No laundry, no grocery shopping, no yard work, no rushing to the bank or post office before they close. When I get home at night I can sit down and read the paper without feeling guilty. We're eating better now that you have time to really cook. I never have to wonder how late you're working. You get all those odd jobs done, such as defrosting the freezer and cleaning out closets and painting woodwork, that we never got around to before. I feel like I'm on vacation."

"It's only fair that I do all that since I'm not working now. But it's a waste of four years of college. I don't intend to make a career out of housework."

"I know. I'd be doing the same things if I were off work. You never know, the economy can be unpredictable. The plant might close or I might lose my job some day, and then we'll switch roles. It doesn't have anything to do with the 'woman should stay at home' syndrome. It's just that having you here is, well, sort of nice."

"The weird thing is that I feel just as busy and tired and pressured now as I did when I was working full time. I still never feel like I have enough hours in the day to accomplish everything. I make lists of my goals for each day and only cross off about half the items by evening. I don't know what's wrong with me."

"You can take a workaholic out of the office, but you can't take the workaholism out of her. Or whatever. You're

so achievement oriented that you'll never get hooked on
soap operas. That's why it doesn't bother me that you're
staying home."

"But I still don't have time for all the things I always
thought I didn't have time for because I was working.
Things like playing piano, reading the Bible and great
literature, cake decorating ... "

"Cake decorating?!"

"Mom's always buying me cake decorating books and
equipment. She clips announcements about cake decorating classes out of the *Suburban Press*. But I've never had
time to get into it."

"Why doesn't she take up cake decorating if it's so
wonderful?"

"She thinks I should be the one in the family to make
fancy cakes for all the special occasions because I was always good in art class."

"Laura, I think your problem is not that you don't have
enough time, but that you always want to do too much."

"But no matter how much I accomplish, I still feel bad
that I'm not helping pay the bills. Intellectually, I know
that everything's okay. But emotionally, I feel like a second-
class citizen because I'm not earning a paycheck. But I
just haven't been able to figure out what I want enough to
know what kind of job to pursue."

"Honey, try not to be so down on yourself. A person's
worth isn't determined by a paycheck. Good grief, look at
the time. I've got to go. We'll talk about this all you want
tonight."

"Tell me the truth, Peter."

"I've got to go," said Peter, gathering up his briefcase,
wallet and keys.

"Am I becoming a boring person?"

"No, of course not."

"You still find me interesting?"

"I still find you interesting. I've got to go. I love you."

He kissed her quickly on his way out the door. Laura
stood in her kitchen and watched him back his Ford

Tempo out of the garage. Then she watched the garage door lower slowly on cue from Peter's electric garage door opener as his car backed out into the street. Then she watched the garage door for a few moments. *Our house looks like nobody's home now,* she thought. *Then again, maybe nobody is.*

Laura gathered up the newspaper, including the want ads she didn't feel up to facing. *I'm too depressed to make a good first impression today.*

Peter's day, she knew, would fly by, filled with meetings and appointments and phone calls. Hers was filled with crossing household tasks off a list. The highlight of the day would be taking a break around noon to read a magazine article. Or maybe she would try to read the rest of one of the three novels she'd begun recently but couldn't seem to finish.

Suddenly she remembered one interesting task that needed doing. *I'd better get my Sunday school lesson out of the way. Peter's always complaining that I have all week to do it but put it off until Saturday night when we should be doing some fun couple thing together.*

□

That Sunday morning as Laura drove herself to church she wondered for the millionth time why she had ever let herself be talked into teaching Sunday school. When she was in college her parents kept pressuring her to take education courses because they thought an education degree was more practical than a plain old English degree. But despite their warnings that she would never find employment, Laura knew in her heart that she lacked the skills necessary to be a good teacher.

"I'm not interesting or witty," Laura had explained to Mrs. Stopenhagen, the Sunday school superintendent who had asked her to take over the youth class when its teacher moved out of state. "I know I'll never be able to control any kids who are discipline problems. I'm not a Bible scholar. And I don't know anything about teenagers.

They're into completely different stuff than I was interested in. We wore ragged blue jeans and long, straight
hair. All they want to do is wear name brand clothing and
weird short hair cuts. It just won't work."

"No one else will take that class. Laura, you're my last
hope. You're young and someone new. The kids will like
you."

Listening to a small voice inside her that whispered,
"Do it. You're not exactly overburdened doing things for
God these days," Laura heard herself say, "Well, okay. I'll
try it for a couple of months and see if I can handle it."

"Great." And with that, Mrs. Stopenhagen handed
Laura a pile of materials.

That was almost two months earlier. Every Sunday
since, Laura had driven to the 9:30 a.m. class knowing she
was a failure. Once she had called a boy who seldom came
an "idiot" for fiddling with a glue bottle and spilling it. A
few times she had even said "shut up," a rude phrase she
had always considered unacceptable. Her worst blunder,
however, was telling a boy whose mother had recently
abandoned his family that he was a "pain in the neck"
when he kept interrupting the lesson.

But perhaps she was most distressed that she had been
unable to prevent the boys, especially one loud-mouthed,
underdeveloped one named Scott, from harassing Judy, a
girl with a slight weight problem. To make it worse, the
boys didn't even bother to find creative insults. They
would just call her "fatso" or "porker." Laura remembered
from her own awkward, chubby youth that such comments
cut deep and instituted a no-calling-anyone-nasty-names-
in-this-class policy. After all, Sunday school should be the
one place a young person could feel safe from persecution.
But the boys usually refused or forgot to obey that rule. In
response, Judy would ignore them or insult them just as
cruelly or threaten physical harm, all to no avail.

As Laura entered the classroom, her mind switched into
high gear. As usual, she was the last person to arrive.

"You're always late!" screamed Tony, who never said anything in a normal tone of voice.

"Yes, I know. It's terrible," said Laura, fumbling with her papers.

"And old!" he added shrilly.

The class had been on this "old" kick since Kristen had thoughtfully pointed out a grey hair on Laura's head a few weeks ago. But Laura had worked with these kids long enough to recognize this teasing as a compliment.

"Now, what about our no-name-calling rule? That especially applies to the teacher," said Laura as she tried to look stern.

"Do we have any crafts today?" asked Kristen.

"No, but we do have a game if we get through our lesson on time," said Laura, hoping the flimsy paper game board and homemade spinner would work. The last game provided in the teacher's packet hadn't withstood the rigors of actual use, and the directions had been ambiguous and caused a huge argument to break out.

"Do we get a prize if we win?"

"Maybe." Laura had forgotten their love of prizes, no matter how insignificant. She began mentally inventorying her purse for some small trinket she could give should there be a clear-cut, undisputed winner.

Laura checked off the attendance on the ragged blue record book. When she first started teaching this class, she had allowed one of the students do this chore, but found it caused too many arguments, so she now did it herself.

Kristen was there, twirling a strand of her long, frizzy hair in her scrawny fingers. She was smart, but lazy. This year she had enrolled in a college prep program but complained constantly about the heavy homework.

Judy was there, too, wearing a jean jacket over a lacy dress. Laura didn't know why she kept coming since the boys in the class verbally abused her. Her family never attended church at all.

Tony, whose large, hot-tempered family attended church regularly and forced Tony to attend, was already mutilating his workbook. He was very bright and had a large vocabulary even though he was such a poor reader that Laura never called on him. Laura assumed he must have learned all those words from hours of television viewing. He was thin and wore hideous black-framed eye glasses. Some part of his awkward body was always in motion.

Heather was also there, applying Chapstick to her lips. She was as close to the perfect child as a seventh grader could be—always neatly dressed and saying positive things about her parents. She once even claimed to enjoy doing dishes. She was perhaps the most disturbed child in the class, Laura thought.

As Laura placed the attendance record book outside the classroom door for Mrs. Stopenhagen to pick up, she saw Scott striding down the hall, swinging both arms. Puberty had not afflicted Scott yet, and he looked like a ten year old even though he was nearly thirteen. Placing a check by his name in the book, Laura told him a lie in hopes they would both believe it: "Oh, good, Scott. I'm glad you're here."

"Sure you are," said Scott, who was used to adults being less than thrilled about his existence. *I've got to be more convincing,* Laura thought. Scott had an older brother and sister, both tall, handsome, popular young people who seldom came to Sunday school.

The class was billed as the "youth" class, but most of the kids were only in junior high. Judy was the oldest, a sophomore.

Herding Scott into the classroom as one might an unruly animal, Laura closed the door and turned to face the class.

"Scott, my man," shouted Tony, thrilled to have another male present. The dynamic duo could cause four times as much mayhem together as they could singly. But while the boys were skilled at overt sabotage of the day's lesson, Laura had learned that the girls were equally expert in surreptitious subversion.

". . . Did you see those ninth grade guys with the Swatch shirts at the game?"

"Yeah, I told my Mom I want one of those for my birthday."

"I'm going to get one when my old man gives me my money next month," said Judy. Her parents were divorced and her father gave her incredible amounts of spending money, which she promptly used to buy faddish clothing and rock music tapes.

"What is a Swatch shirt?" asked Laura.

Eyes rolled. "They're a really great shirt. I don't know how to describe it," said Kristen as though she were explaining something to a toddler.

"The sweatshirts cost forty dollars," said Judy.

"You can't be serious," said Laura, realizing that once again the girls had managed to sidetrack the lesson.

"That's not that much for a good shirt," said Heather.

As was often the case in these encounters with the younger generation, Laura couldn't believe her ears. She had a list of the youngsters' addresses and phone numbers and knew none of them lived in the wealthy parts of town. Some of their families didn't even own telephones, and they had to give her the number of a nearby neighbor or relative. Most of their parents were not much older than Laura and Peter. Laura knew that one of the families was receiving food stamps. How could they even conceive of a forty dollar sweatshirt?

Somehow, Laura feebly got the lesson back on track. This quarter they were studying the Old Testament prophets. Laura herself was starting to get bored with it. The story was always the same, even though the Sunday school materials highlighted a different concept each week. The prophets spoke God's word to the stubborn people. The prophets were unpopular. The people either ignored them or persecuted them. The people eventually repented. God always gave them another chance.

Today's lesson was on Jonah.

"God not only gave the people of Nineveh a chance to

stop doing evil and follow God, but he also gave Jonah a second chance. What does this story mean to us today?" asked Laura, reading the question from the teacher's guide. *Maybe I got off on the wrong foot by letting them call me Laura instead of Mrs. Morton.*

Silence.

"Surely this story has some meaning for you guys. What do you think this tells us about the nature of God?"

Again, no one ventured an opinion.

"Kristen, what do you think?"

"I guess that, well, I don't know. I guess that God is love." *Always a safe answer.*

"Come on, you guys. This is an important concept. The answer is very simple and obvious. It means that even when we really mess up—like Jonah did by running away from God or the people of Nineveh did by being so rotten—God still loves us and wants to forgive us and give us a second chance."

"This is boring," whined Tony. As usual, Laura ignored such inappropriate remarks, but Tony took some pleasure in the irritated arch of her eyebrows.

"Believing this will really help you in your everyday life," said Laura, abandoning her teaching materials. "When you get depressed and feel worthless because you've made some big mistake that you can't fix, remember that God still loves you. If you're really sorry, he wants to forgive you, no matter how bad you've been. Knowing this will help you keep your sanity."

"Laura, do you believe everything you teach us?" asked Scott slyly while nonchalantly tearing off pieces of scotch tape and wading them up into little balls.

"Yes, I do, Scott," said Laura, knowing this was a trick of some kind.

"Then how come you're insane?"

The class exploded with laughter. Laura smirked.

"Now what about our rule not to insult people in our class?"

"I thought you wanted us to ask questions," said Scott innocently.

"I don't think that was an honest question," said Laura, trying to be incensed but still rather amused at his comment and pleased because it meant he had to be listening at least a little bit. "Good grief, why do I even dignify your derogatory comments with a reply? Now, can anybody tell me what we were discussing, or trying to discuss? It wasn't really a discussion, because to call something a discussion implies that more than one person is involved in the conversation, and I don't think any of you were listening."

Silence.

At last, Heather said, "God always gives us a second chance. But you know . . . "

"Yes, Heather," Laura encouraged her, excited to at last be on the verge of an in-depth discussion like the ones prescribed by the teacher's guide.

"Well, I don't think God should have given the people of that city another chance, I mean, if they were so rotten. He should have punished them, like Jonah said."

"Class, what do you think about Heather's suggestion?"

"Yeah, he should've blown them away," said Scott as he and Tony launched into a series of noises that sounded like bombs exploding.

"Okay, so Tony and Scott agree with Heather. Does anybody have any idea why God changed his mind about the people of Nineveh?" asked Laura.

No one responded, but Tony and Scott continued to make bombing and machine gun noises.

"Well, Heather, you're right that the people were truly rotten and deserved to be punished. And as human beings, we like to see the bad guys get what they have coming to them, even if they are really sorry for what they've done. But lucky for us, God isn't like us. He can forgive even the worst sinner who honestly repents."

Tony raised his hand, which was unusual in itself.

Could he actually be wanting to participate in a class discussion? Laura wondered.

"Laura, it's time."

Laura looked at her watch. He was right. "Well, that's it for today. Next week we'll be studying the prophet Hosea . . ." But her class was already fleeing. Laura sighed as she piled up her papers and gathered the student books. She was glad the class was over for another week and felt guilty for feeling that way. *I'm just not getting through. I'm not helping anybody,* she was thinking as Judy, who had lingered behind the stampede, hesitantly approached her.

"Laura?"

"Yes, Judy," said Laura, her heart quickening. Could this be the beginning of a meaningful teacher-student interaction? "You know the part in today's lesson about God forgiving us no matter how bad we mess up?"

"Yes."

"Well, I've really, really messed up, and I don't think God or my parents or anyone will be able to forgive me."

"Judy, what do you mean? Are you in some kind of trouble?"

"Yes, I'm in big trouble, and it's all my fault." Judy walked over to the classroom window and watched the people migrating from their cars in the parking lot to the church doors. "If I tell you, you promise you won't tell anyone?"

"You can trust me, Judy. I won't tell anyone if you don't want me to."

"I just found out this week that I'm pregnant. I used one of those drug store tests."

"Oh, no, that's terrible."

"I just can't believe it. I never thought this would happen to me."

"How old are you, Judy? Sixteen? Are you going to marry the father?"

"Fifteen. No, he don't want anything to do with me. But

I wouldn't marry him even if he did." Judy turned to face
Laura, tears starting to roll down her round face.

"Have you told your parents?"

"Yeah. I told my Mom right away. She's always been sort
of like a girlfriend to me more than a mom. I didn't think
she'd get that mad. I mean, she lets me stay out as late as
I want and do anything I want. Anyway, she called my dad
and he came over, and they both yelled at me for an hour.
They kept saying stuff like, 'How could you be so stupid?'
and 'I never raised you to get pregnant at fifteen.' My mom
said I should've asked her and she would have got me on
birth control. But I never planned to do it. It just sort of
happened."

"Oh, Judy, that's terrible."

"See, I was going out with this guy named Ronnie. He's
a junior. And he said I was chicken and that I didn't love
him cause I wouldn't go all the way. And he swore to me
that he's had sex with seven other girls and none of them
got pregnant so he had to be sterile."

"Oh, Judy, guys have been using those lines on girls as
long as there've been guys."

"You think I'm pretty stupid, too, don't you?" said Judy,
sitting down on a metal folding chair and hiding her face
in her hands.

"No, I just think you made a big mistake. Everybody
makes mistakes. Now you have to decide what to do and
live with the consequences." Laura awkwardly took Judy's
hand. She could hear the organ in the sanctuary playing
the processional. Peter would be pacing in the narthex,
wondering where she was. "Judy," Laura continued, "try to
look at the good that can come out of this. It will be hard,
but whether you decide to keep the baby or give it up so
some loving family can adopt it, you can know that you
brought a new life into the world."

"That's the worst part of it," Judy said as an agonizing
grimace twisted her face. "My parents are taking me to
have an abortion. They say I'm too young to have a baby.
Mom made an appointment with her doctor for this week.

But there's a baby inside me, isn't there, Laura? I don't
want to kill my baby."

Laura absolutely did not know what to say. In her
youth, a girl who got "in trouble" would almost always
marry the young man, even though these marriages often
ended in divorce. *Times are changing,* thought Laura.

"My mom says it's just a little bloody speck now, that's
it's not a baby yet, but I think it's a baby. I don't know
what to do. I don't have anywhere to go. I have to live with
my mom. I know I can't raise a baby by myself. I don't
even want to, really. I don't want to be tied down with a
baby. But I don't want to kill it, if it is a baby. How could
God ever forgive me for that? Abortion is murder, isn't it? I
just don't know what to do."

Suddenly Laura had an inspiration. "Judy, you're not
the only person who's ever made this mistake, believe me.
There's all kinds of organizations in this city to help
people in bad situations like you. I've read about a good
one, called the Pregnancy Problem Center, that can help
you. Let's go to the church office and look up their number
right now."

Taking Judy by the hand, she led her downstairs. As
they crossed the back of the narthex on their way to the
church office, Laura saw Peter, pacing as she knew he
would be. He saw her and raced over to them.

"Laura, what happened? Church has started. I've been
waiting here twenty minutes for you."

"I'm sorry, Peter, we have a sort of emergency here.
Please go sit down; I'll be there in a minute."

"An emergency? What is it? Can I help?"

"No. Please just go get us a pew. I'll be right in."

Judy had gone ahead to the church office and was waiting outside the door. She was no longer visibly crying, although from time to time a half-stifled sob would shake
her plump body. Laura hurried over to her and opened the
door as hearty male laughter came from inside.

In the office, a couple of middle-aged men were counting

the offering money on a large desk while a third man sat on the couch.

"Excuse us a moment," said Laura while Judy huddled behind her. "We need to use the telephone book."

"What's your problem?" asked one of the men, scowling at the two females through thick glasses.

"We just need to find an important phone number," said Laura resolutely. She had always noticed that these ushers left with the offering plates after the collection and never reappeared in the sanctuary until after the sermon.

"You know, church has already started," said the grey haired man who was lounging on the couch.

"Yes, we know," said Laura, offering no further explanation.

"Here it is," said the other money-counter as he hoisted the thick Cincinnati white pages onto his large belly. "What number do you need?" he asked as he began flipping through it.

"If you don't mind, we'll look it up ourselves," said Laura, not knowing what else to say but fearing this would only pique their interest. The portly man eyed her skeptically as he slowly handed the book over to her. As soon as she could reach it, Laura snatched it from him. She and Judy turned and placed the phone book on top of a low shelf on the wall behind them. With their backs to the three nosy men, Laura nervously paged through the book until she found the agency's listing. Fishing some paper and an ink pen out of her purse, she wrote the number down and handed it to Judy, all without saying a word. As they turned around to hand the phone book back to the men, they found all three were staring at them intently.

"Find what you need?" asked the other money handler, a lanky man with a shiny bald head and a mouth that permanently turned down at the corners.

"Yes, thank you," said Laura. She opened the door and she and Judy, whose eyes were red and swollen, slipped out.

"Whew. That was like the inquisition," said Laura as soon as they were outside, back in the narthex.

"Huh?" said Judy, who was staring at the phone number on the little scrap of paper as though she were in a trance.

I guess that scene didn't upset Judy as much as it did me because she's used to being treated like a child, since she still is one, thought Laura.

"Now, call that number when you get home. I know the people there can help you. You're in a difficult situation and I'm really not competent to advise you what to do. I don't want to undermine your parents' authority, but I think you should consider some other options besides abortion. But without your parents' support those other options will be very, very difficult for you."

"Do you know any of the people at this place?"

"No, but I've read articles about it and heard other people talk about it. Their office is on Glenway Avenue at Prout's Corner. Their entire purpose is to help girls who are pregnant find ways to avoid having abortions. Now, you promise me you'll call them?"

"I will. I better get going. I never stay for church and my mom will wonder what happened to me."

"Take care of yourself, Judy," said Laura. "I'll see you next week? You'll let me know what happens?"

"Yeah, I'll try to be here. Bye."

With that, Judy slipped quietly out the heavy wooden church doors. Laura watched the huge door close behind Judy's stout, lace and denim clad form, then tiptoed across the narthex and sneaked through the glass doors into the sanctuary. She settled into the pew beside Peter as the organist began the chords of the final hymn. Peter looked peeved. "I'll tell you all about it when we get home," she whispered in his ear.

□

"Why, why, why, do people like Judy, who are totally unprepared for parenthood, get pregnant while people like us, who pray for a child daily, remain barren?" Laura was pacing the kitchen floor, gesturing with her hands. Peter watched her from his chair at the kitchen table, his elbows resting on the table and his head in his hands. Sections of the Sunday *Enquirer* were strewn amid the remains of the fast food meal they'd picked up on the way home from church.

"I guess a person's ability to conceive is inversely proportional to their desire to be pregnant," he observed glumly. "So anyway, do you think she'll call that agency?"

"Oh, I'm sure she will. I know they'll help her. I've heard nothing but good things about the Pregnancy Problem Center. They're experts at helping young girls find alternatives to abortion. They'll help her get baby clothes and things if she decides to keep the baby or help arrange adoption if she decides to give the baby up. It's staffed by Christians from various denominations."

"Sounds like a good outfit."

"I just didn't know what to say to her. It will be so hard for her to keep her baby, or even endure nine months of pregnancy and give it up for adoption, if her parents aren't on her side, since she has to live with them. She's only fifteen. It's a horrible, rotten shame."

"I'm proud of you for trying to help her. I'm sorry I haven't always been sympathetic to your need to teach Sunday school. You're right—it is important, and I'm glad you've stuck with it. You really have a chance to make a difference in someone's life."

"I don't know. On one hand, I'm glad Judy came to me and that I could help her. But on the other hand, I feel like I've failed miserably."

"What do you mean?"

"If I'd done a better job, maybe she wouldn't have gotten in this situation in the first place."

"Now you can't blame yourself. She has a rotten family life. Our culture bombards kids with the message that sex is great and wonderful and everybody's doing it with everybody. The causes of teenage pregnancy are complex. The experts don't even agree on why there's so much of it."

"I don't know about all the reasons for teenage pregnancy in America, but I know why Judy got pregnant. She has a very low self-opinion. Some guy comes along and no matter how much of a scum wad he is, he makes her feel, even if just for a little bit, like she's attractive and loved and worthwhile. He's just using her, but because of her pent-up need for love, she sees their relationship as a great romance. And because of her low self-esteem she thinks she'll never get another guy if she loses him, so she gives in to whatever he wants."

"I wonder why she didn't use birth control?"

"Because that would destroy the romance of it all. It would also mean that she 'planned' to have sex, which she thinks would make her a bad person. Much better, she thinks, to just get carried away by the passions of the moment. Besides, kids think nothing bad will ever happen to them. That's why teenagers take so many risks. But I should've been able to save Judy from this terrible situation."

"Will you stop blaming yourself? It's not in any way your fault."

"I could have done more to boost her self-esteem. That might have given her the confidence to say no. I should have talked about sex in class—you know, tried to teach them the Christian perspective. I'm afraid of the topic, and they seem so young and immature, so I never go near the subject. Besides, that's their parents' job, and the parents might get really mad and make their kids quit coming if I start talking about sex in Sunday school. But still, I should've risked it. Maybe I could have saved Judy."

"You couldn't be expected to save Judy. How could you expect to undo everything that she had going against her?"

"You're right. I couldn't save Judy, but I should've been able to introduce her to the Person who could."

"There you go putting yourself down again. No one in that church could do any better job of teaching those kids than you."

"I didn't mean someone else in the church. I meant
Jesus. He could save Judy."

"But what do you think you're doing? You teach the kids
about Jesus every week. It's not your fault if they ignore
his invitation."

"It's one thing to teach them the facts about Jesus.
What I need to do is to bring them to him. I don't think I
ever do that."

"I don't know what you mean. You've done everything a
Sunday school teacher can humanly be expected to do for
those kids."

"Precisely. That's why I've failed them."

"Will you get off this failed kick? Sex is fun, kids are interested in it, and they're going to do it. Period. The problem is that puberty starts earlier and earlier due to good
nutrition or something like that. Our culture wants kids to
wait longer and longer to get married because it takes a
person until at least age twenty-two to graduate from college and start a career. Look, your grandmother and your
Aunt Lucy both got married at sixteen. And my Grandpa
went to Detroit at seventeen and got a job; he was support-
ing a family at nineteen. No nineteen year old could do
that today. None of these things are your fault, so I don't
see how you can say you failed."

"Oh, let's just drop it. I know the basketball game you
want to watch is on. I'm okay. Don't worry about me."

"Are you sure?"

"Yes, I'm okay."

"You know I think you're the best."

"Thanks, Peter."

"You know, if the Celtics can beat L.A. today they can
win the whole thing," Peter explained as he gathered up
the Sunday newspaper and headed for the living room.

"That'd be great," said Laura as she stood and stared
out the kitchen's back door.

Chapter 11

Mount Echo

◻ ◼ ◻

Laura stood at the back door several minutes longer, watching a squirrel run nimbly along their back yard's privacy fence. She listened to the "sportsroar," as she called the noise of the crowds and announcers at sporting events, coming from the television in their living room. *I wonder what happens when a person has a nervous breakdown,* she thought. *Could I be having one now? Nah, I never let myself go enough to do that. I always have to be in control.*

The beautiful early summer afternoon was at odds with her despondent mood. She heard the breeze ruffle the tops of the oak and maple trees around their house while puddles of sunlight warmed the bright green grass. *Maybe a stroll outdoors will improve my state of mind*, she thought as she turned and walked through the house to the living room.

"I think I'm going for a hike, Peter. It's a gorgeous day and I don't feel like being cooped up in the house."

"Will you be upset if I stay here and watch the game? It's the big one."

"They're all the big one," Laura said, laughing and bending over the couch to kiss Peter on the cheek. This was an old family joke. His mother said that when Peter was a boy he was always begging to watch some kind of ball

game on television, arguing that it was "the big one," an
important game that could not be missed. Somehow, every
game on the schedule became "the big one."

"You sure you don't mind?" asked Peter, his eyes glued
to the television screen.

"No, I want a chance to think and clear my head. A nice,
long walk will help put me in a better frame of mind."

"Well, enjoy yourself, honey."

Laura bent over and hugged and kissed Peter again,
then left through the front door. As she walked down their
front steps, noticing with dismay some cracks that needed
patching, she decided to head toward Mount Echo, a small
city park about five blocks from their home. As she walked
down the sidewalk in her blue jeans, Reeboks and a yellow
button down oxford cloth shirt, her feet found their own
rhythm while her mind raced. As was her habit, Laura
composed her thoughts as though God were eavesdropping
while she expounded before a large group of unsym-
pathetic listeners.

*Why did God ever allow humans to become involved in
reproduction? He should have maintained complete control
of the process. That way God could make babies appear
only in families that are completely mature and ready for
them. But then, maybe no family would fit that description. Anyway, the act of reproduction, of creating a totally
new human being, is the most awesome, godlike thing we
miserable humans do, and yet we take it for granted.
People get pregnant even though they have absolutely none
of the resources needed to nurture the fragile new life they
create.*

*And yet, for some reason, God apparently wants us
humans to play this role. Reproduction is almost a physical need, like hunger or thirst. I ache to have a baby.
Funny how all my life I just assumed I'd have kids but
never seriously considered it until one day, pow! I felt this
intense desire to be a mother. Suddenly, nothing else in life
seems as important.*

This longing has to be a God-given gift, because if people

*approached the thing rationally, the species would die out.
Kids are expensive. They disrupt your career. They drool
and throw food on the floor. They wake a person up in the
middle of the night and get sick at inconvenient times. Not
to mention the months of nausea, swollen ankles and un-
sightly weight gain that precede childbirth, and the terrible pain and messiness of birth itself. I mean, I get
grossed out by cold pizza and bad hangnails, but I want a
baby. So here I am, stuck with these instinctual maternal
urgings and no baby. Why?*

As Laura carried on her inner dialogue, Price Hill's
cracked and uneven sidewalks brought her to the crumbling, massive stone steps of the gate to Mount Echo Park.
She could feel her legs working hard as she walked up the
steep sidewalk that lead to Mount Echo's lookout point. *I
used to think that God carefully placed each new baby on
earth, but I don't anymore. Why would God send babies
into abusive households while loving families remain barren? No, I think God gives us humans this tremendous
power for some unfathomable reason, to use wisely or to totally mess up, just as we do with all the remarkable
abilities he's given us.*

As Laura reached the top of the hill, she glimpsed the
Ohio River far below. The city had, uncharacteristically,
spent money the previous year to fix up Price Hill's little
gem of a park, so the lookout had new concrete benches
and a fancy black wrought iron fence. Meanwhile, a local
civic group had been doing some serious gardening, and
geraniums, marigolds, larkspur, cock's comb and other
summer flowers bloomed riotously in little plots
everywhere.

Laura walked to the edge of the lookout and leaned
trustingly against the sturdy wrought iron fence. Looking
down she could see lazy barges on the wide river below
and downtown nestled in the valley at the river's bend.
She had always thought this west side panorama was the
best view in Cincinnati, her east side friends' opinions not-
withstanding.

The park looks so much better today than it did two years ago when I used to come here, thought Laura. *But then, everything was uglier two years ago when I came here with Andrew.*

Mount Echo, only a few minutes from Northwest Press, had hosted several of her rendezvous with Andrew. When Peter found out about the affair, Laura told him everything, including the fact that she and Andrew used to meet at Mount Echo. Consequently, she and Peter stopped visiting the little park because anything associated with that period in their lives was too painful to acknowledge. Laura couldn't even drive by the park without cringing at the memory of the loathsome thing she had done.

Right after the discovery, she and Peter had talked about the affair ad nauseam—the reasons why it had happened, what they should do to improve their marriage, where they had each made mistakes. But now that it was behind them, they tacitly agreed never to mention the affair or even refer to it in the vaguest of terms.

Oh, Lord. How did I ever let it happen? You know I've been involved in some pretty stupid things, but that one even disgusts me. I can imagine how you, a God of holiness, must feel about it. And to think that three times a week for four years of college I stared at the phrase "Holiness Unto the Lord" written over the pipe organ in our college chapel. Not only have I not followed your holy ways, I'm not even decent. Lots of my pagan friends would never, ever treat someone as deceitfully as I treated my beloved Peter. And he is my beloved. He's not perfect, but Lord, you know how good and kind he is. And he forgave me. I can't believe he forgave me and can still love me. I'm thankful, but it almost makes me feel more worthless than ever.

Laura sat down on one of the new concrete benches and looked through the iron bars at the river winding peacefully below. She didn't want to, but some morbid curiosity made her turn her head and arch her neck to see whether "their" bench was still there. It was. About twenty feet

beyond the new concrete the old, green park bench still sat
at the base of a huge oak tree.

Just the sight of the bench made Laura's skin crawl.
Seeing it sitting there in the secluded, cool shade made the
misery of her affair seem very, very recent.

She tried to picture Peter sitting on that bench, holding
hands with—kissing was out of the question—some
strange woman, but she couldn't. In the many books and
articles on marital infidelity she'd studied during and
after her affair, Laura had read that people who engage in
an extramarital affair are often extremely suspicious of
their faithful spouse. But Laura had never worried that
Peter would stray. What she had done was so abominable
that she could never conceive of any morally competent
person doing the same thing, let alone good, kind, loving
Peter.

*Sometimes Peter seems self-centered, but he is really just
trying to be honest, like we agreed to do. I still hide my feelings and desires when I think they will appear selfish or
inappropriate, while Peter usually has the courage to
reveal what he is thinking or feeling, no matter how it
looks.*

Just as a streetlight attracts condemned moths, something about the bench drew Laura toward it. She walked
over and stood in front of it, looking at it as though it were
a witness who was testifying against her in court.

*Why don't you just be honest, for once in your life. Quit
worrying about that internal audience you always play to.
Lord, what's wrong with me?*

A scripture verse, "Be still and know that I am Lord,"
came to her mind. *Yes, Lord, I'm listening.* Laura sat down
in the dirt in front of the bench—to sit on it would have
been unthinkable—and stared at the cursed object. From
her vantage point on the ground, it loomed huge and
foreboding over her. The curved wrought iron arm rests
reminded her of an enormous scale of justice. Another
verse entered her head: "You have been weighed in the
scales and found wanting."

Lord, I've failed you. My own efforts to be good are so feeble, and I have botched my life up so completely. I know your commandments are designed to help us live happy, fulfilled lives, but I totally ignored one of the big ten. Actually, I disobeyed two, because I had to tell a lot of lies. How could I do that? I knew better.

She sat in the dirt a while longer, then walked to the edge of the concrete, where the iron fence also ended, and looked down. Below her was a steep embankment covered with a few scrubby trees and bushes, their roots mostly exposed by the recent excavation. At the bottom of the precipice she noted a pile of jagged concrete, bricks and broken glass, half hidden by the undergrowth.

A person could jump off this edge and kill herself. Of course, I would never do that, but if I did, it wouldn't be much of a loss. Peter could find someone worthy of him. My Sunday school kids could get a real teacher. My mother would lose her greatest thorn in the flesh. Probably the only one who would miss me is Grandma, and she probably wouldn't like me if she knew the horrible things I've done in my life. But of course I'd never do anything crazy like jump.

Laura hung onto the end of the iron fence and dangled herself near the edge of the bluff. *The city really should do something about this dangerous drop off. If I fell, I wonder if Peter would sue the city? Nah, he would never even think of anything like that. Of course, I'd never even consider suicide, although it would be ironic to get to heaven before Grandma. I could greet her as she entered the pearly gates, "What took you so long, Grandma?" We'd laugh. But I guess if I committed suicide I'd end up on the wrong side of the pearly gates. Besides, if Grandma can hang on to life so fiercely, I shouldn't throw it away. . . . I wonder what makes her hang on to life so tenaciously. Even when her doctors give up on her, she always somehow pulls through. It's like she's waiting to do one more thing before she leaves. Or, Lord, maybe you're giving her one more chance to do something. To do what?*

Laura sighed and pulled herself away from the bluff and back to the safety of the concrete sidewalk. She sat on one of the concrete benches and resumed contemplating the laconic river.

I know the main reason why I couldn't fling myself over now. What if this is the month? What if there is a little life inside me right now, depending on me for his or her survival? Oh, Lord, I can't give up hope. I want to hold my baby so much. Come to think of it, maybe that's why Grandma can't let go. She wants to hold the baby she lost before she goes gently into that dark night. Something about holding a baby is redeeming. Maybe that's why I want a baby so badly, Lord. I want to be redeemed.

Laura glanced at her watch. She had been at the park nearly an hour, oblivious to the many people who had come, taken photos of the view and left during that time. Slowly, she rose and began walking back to the sidewalk that would lead her out of the park. But as she was leaving, she turned to look at the evil green bench one last time.

As she did, she remembered one summer evening when she had told Peter she was working late. Instead, she and Andrew had gone to a motel across the river in northern Kentucky, ostensibly to have some place to talk—"renting privacy" as Andrew had called it. But somehow they ended up doing more than talking.

That's it, isn't it, Lord? You know it, even though I won't admit it, not even to myself. You know about the evil in my heart that makes my affair look like a golden moment. Oh, Lord, I feel so guilty. How can I be worthwhile? Why should I even be allowed to live?

Another verse, filed away a zillion Sundays ago, popped into her head: "If we claim to be without sin, we deceive ourselves and the truth is not in us." *Boy, that's certainly accurate.* "If we confess our sins, he is faithful and just and will forgive us our sins and purify us from all unrighteousness." *If anyone ever needed purifying, it's me.*

Laura stopped, turned around and walked back to the

bench of wickedness (as it would have been called, she was sure, if her story had been recorded in the Old Testament). *Lord, you know my darkest, innermost secrets. I can even hide my sins from myself, but not from you. You know what I considered doing two years ago.* Tears welled up in Laura's eyes. She stared at the bench so intensely that it almost seemed to move.

You know that I am capable of the most unspeakable sin a human being can commit. Laura began to cry softly, tears trickling down her face. A ragtag young couple walked by, the girl with her arm around his waist and he with his hand in the back pocket of her blue jeans. They stared at Laura as though she were a lunatic, but Laura didn't notice them.

I thought I was pregnant that month. I always think I'm pregnant. But that month I feared being pregnant. I dreaded it. Why? You know, Lord. It's too awful to remember. If I had been pregnant that month, I wouldn't have known who the father was—Peter or Andrew. How could I have put myself in such a deplorable situation? But even that wasn't the worst of it.

Laura tried to quiet her mind, but just as the tongue probes a decayed tooth, she could not stop the flow of her prayer-like thoughts.

You know I decided that if I were pregnant I would get rid of the baby, destroy it before it could be born, through no fault of its own, to such uncertain parentage. You saw me look up the numbers of places that do such things in the Yellow Pages. You heard me scheme to have it done without letting Peter know. You know, Lord, that I was capable of killing my own baby.

Tears now poured down her face as she sniffed her running nose. *Oh, Lord, I've just confessed my most dreadful sin, for which I am incredibly sorry. Please, please, Lord, forgive me and give me peace.*

She stumbled back toward the concrete benches, sat on one for a few moments until she felt somewhat composed and headed for home.

□

That Tuesday night as Laura returned from a Sunday school education committee meeting, Peter met her at the door.

"Judy called while you were out. I took her number. She sounded upset, but she wouldn't tell me anything."

"Oh, no. I wonder what's happened," said Laura as she took the paper with the phone number on it and flew into the den. This was the first time any of her Sunday school kids had ever called her at home.

She nervously dialed the number and let it ring several times. She was about to hang up when a small voice answered.

"Hello?"

"Judy, is that you?"

"Hi, Laura. Thanks for calling. I wanted to talk to you while my mom was gone."

"What's happened? Are you okay?"

"Well, I wanted to talk to you about it. I feel terrible."

"That's what I'm here for."

"I had the abortion today. I didn't want it, but my mom took me. Even the people at the doctor's office told me that it was the best thing to do. I don't know, maybe they're right. I just don't know what to think."

"Oh, Judy, you poor thing. What did the people at the Pregnancy Problem Center tell you?"

"Well, I sort of didn't call them."

"You didn't? Why not?"

"Well, I almost did. But I didn't know anyone there and I was afraid to. I thought they might tell my mom I called. I didn't know what they might do. I don't see how they could do anything to help me and my baby anyway." As Judy said "baby" her voice cracked and she began weeping loudly.

"Judy, if I'd known you wouldn't call them I would have taken you there myself."

"That's okay. There's nothing they could do. There's

nothing anyone could do," said Judy between sobs. "I'm too
young to raise a baby by myself, and if I gave it up for
adoption, who knows what terrible things might happen to
it. Laura . . . "

"Yes, Judy."

"Am I a murderer?"

"No, Judy, you're not the murderer. You're just a very
young girl in a terrible situation."

"But I feel awful."

"Well, I'll tell you what the Bible tells us to do when we
feel awful. Confess—tell—God all your sins and ask him to
forgive them. He can wipe the slate clean so we can start
over again. No matter what we do, he will always forgive
us. He wants to forgive us."

"Are you sure God could forgive a murderer?"

"God can forgive any kind of sin. Just pray to him and
ask him for forgiveness."

"I'll try to pray, Laura," said Judy. She had stopped
crying and was sniffing noisily now. "I hear my mom pulling into the driveway. I've got to go. I'll talk to you later."
With that she hung up.

Feeling numb, Laura walked into the living room where
Peter was sitting on the couch, the sports page folded in
his lap.

"So she went ahead and had the abortion," said Peter,
who had listened to the conversation.

"Yeah," said Laura as she sank into the overstuffed
chair.

"She didn't call the pregnancy crisis place?"

"No. She was afraid to. I should have taken her there. I
should have done something, been more involved. She really needed me and I let her down."

"Now don't start blaming yourself for that."

"She asked me if I thought she was a murderer."

"You gave her a good answer."

"I've always thought abortion is murder. In this case, I
really don't think Judy is the murderer, but I wouldn't say
the same thing about her parents and the so-called doctor

who actually did the horrible deed, or me, who didn't care enough or take the time to give Judy all the support she needed. Anyway, I tried to tell her it doesn't matter what she's done, that God forgives all who earnestly repent and are heartily sorry for these our misdoings and so forth."

"I thought you explained the concept very well, as well as anyone could explain a deep theological concept on the spur of the moment."

"I don't know," said Laura. "I'm exhausted. I'm going to bed."

"I'm going to stay up a little longer. There's one more article in the paper I want to read."

"Goodnight," said Laura, kissing Peter on the head. As she slowly walked up the stairs she thought, *I can explain it to poor Judy. I believe it, intellectually at least, but I can't feel forgiven. I've confessed my deepest sin to God, but I still feel terrible. What's left to do? I'm sorry, I'm sorry, I'm sorry. It doesn't seem to work. I still feel unfit for motherhood, or anything else, come to think of it.*

She had reached the top of the stairs and turned into their bedroom. She couldn't wait to get into her nightgown and fall exhausted into bed.

Chapter 12

The Quickening Ray

□ ■ □

On Thursday of that week it rained all morning, but the afternoon sullenly allowed a little sunlight to break through now and then. Looking out the kitchen window, Laura thought that despite the gloom, the rain had made the neighborhood look clean and fresh.

Barefoot and wearing a pink sweatsuit, Laura sat at one of the pressed-back oak chairs at the kitchen table contemplating her list of objectives for the day. It was two o'clock in the afternoon and so far she had only managed to cross off three items. Rainy days always made her feel cozy and lazy.

None of the jobs left on her list were particularly appealing, so Laura was using a decision-avoiding device she had learned from Elaine: When facing too many projects of equal importance, number each item, roll some dice and perform the task that corresponds to the number that turns up. Laura kept a small blue die pilfered from some seldom used game in a kitchen drawer for this purpose. She fished the tiny object out from the tangle of scissors and rubber bands and rolled it across the round oak kitchen table.

Let's see. Five. That would be organizing the horrible

cupboard. Peter called the cabinet under their old fashioned porcelain sink the "horrible cupboard" because it was haphazardly filled with bulky items such as colanders, graters and funnels. Since Peter usually dried dishes while Laura washed them, he had to endure these objects spilling out on the floor whenever he opened the door to put something away. Each time this happened, Laura would promise to someday organize the precarious jumble.

I don't think I'm in the mood to tackle that. I think I'll roll one more time. Laura tossed the die across the table again. It bounced merrily and landed on three.

Three. Prepare Sunday school lesson. Well, at least I'll be so proud of myself for not putting it off until the last minute, as per usual.

Laura traipsed into the den and dragged her Sunday school materials and Bible from the library table's bottom shelf. The den's lone, tall, narrow window wasn't letting in much of the gloomy afternoon daylight, so she migrated to the living room where the front door's beveled glass and the big bay window permitted the scarce sunshine to filter through their lace curtains. To prevent squandering earth's precious natural resources on her homely activities, she had a policy of not turning on electric lights unless absolutely necessary.

Laura plopped down on the Queen Anne sofa and spread her Sunday school materials on the antique mahogany coffee table. *Hmmmm. This week's lesson is about Hosea. Thank goodness this is the last Old Testament prophet we're studying this quarter. I'm so tired of the prophets, I can imagine how bored the kids must be. Okay, Hosea. Let's see if we can find anything new and improved to say about the wayward people of Israel this week.*

Laura read the Scripture synopsis in the teacher's manual. *Oh, yeah. Hosea was the one with the unfaithful wife—I thought that was Joel. I never was any good at remembering the minor prophets. The teacher's manual says Hosea's adulterous wife "served as a metaphor for the*

*people of Israel who abandoned their belief in God to wor-
ship the pagan idols of the surrounding cultures." Too bad.
human nature hasn't improved in the intervening centuries.*

She decided to look up the little book of Hosea and read
it for herself. *It's somewhere toward the end of the Old Testament. Ah, here it is.*

When she reached chapter six, verse four struck her as
an apt description of her own relationship with God: ". . .
Your love is like the morning mist, like the early dew that
disappears." *God sure knows his human beings. I started
out with so much enthusiasm for Christianity, but now my
relationship with God consists of performing little chores
for him out of a sense of obligation.*

She recognized verse six of that chapter as the well-
spring of many a sermon: "For I desire mercy, not sacrifice,
and acknowledgment of God rather than burnt offerings."
*Guess you're not too impressed with all the little churchy
things I do to make myself look good.*

Fascinated, she kept reading. In chapter eight, beginning with verse two, she read, "Israel cries out to me, 'O
our God, we acknowledge you!' But Israel has rejected
what is good; an enemy will pursue him. They set up kings
without my consent; they choose princes without my approval. With their silver and gold they make idols for themselves to their own destruction." *I've chosen a lot of princes
without God's approval or consent. Now verse seven
describes how I feel: "They sow the wind and reap the
whirlwind." How can something written so many centuries
ago so accurately describe how I feel? It's uncanny.*

The sermons on Hosea were forgotten and Laura read
on, moved by the poetry. In chapter ten she read, ". . . it is
time to seek the Lord, until he comes and showers
righteousness on you. But you have planted wickedness,
and have reaped evil, you have eaten the fruit of decep-
tion. Because you have depended on your own strength
and on your many warriors, the roar of battle will rise
against your people, so that all your fortresses will be
devastated. . . ." *I have definitely eaten the fruit of decep-*

*tion and depended on my own strength too many times.
The fruit is vile tasting and my fortresses are quite devastated. Dear Lord, this is me.*

Tears began to flow down Laura's face as she read chapter eleven. "When Israel was a child, I loved him, and out
of Egypt I called my son. But the more I called Israel, the
further they went from me." *The more I've felt you calling
me, the harder I have run away from you, Lord. I guess I've
been afraid of what I would have to give up. How can you
stomach us short-sighted, ungrateful humans, Lord?*

"My heart is changed within me; all my compassion is
aroused. I will not carry out my fierce anger, nor devastate
Ephraim again. For I am God, and not man—the Holy
One among you. I will not come in wrath." *So that's how
you stand us.*

Laura continued reading as the prophet described
Israel's sins and the Lord's terrible fury at the wayward
nation's faithlessness. But as she read chapter fourteen,
the last chapter, she dropped to her knees in their living
room, burying her head in the tasteful damask upholstery
of her Queen Anne sofa.

"Return, O Israel, to the Lord your God. Your sins have
been your downfall! Take words with you and return to
the Lord. Say to him: 'Forgive all our sins and receive us
graciously, that we may offer the fruit of our lips . . . . We
will never again say 'Our gods' to what our own hands
have made, for in you the fatherless find compassion.'

"I will heal their waywardness and love them freely, for
my anger has turned away from them."

*Oh Lord, my sins are certainly my downfall. Please for-
give me and accept my praise. I will never again trust in
what I can do myself, but in your mercy. Thank you, Lord,
for not only offering me the intellectual gift of forgiveness—
I know you have the power to forgive sins—but for offering
to heal me and love me freely. Oh Lord, please heal me.*

As Laura knelt in the dim living room, her eyes tightly
closed and her tear streaked face hidden in her hands, she
felt as though God were surrounding her with love. It was

not so much an emotional or intellectual realization as it
was a purely physical sensation. She felt as though the
very arm of God were around her shoulder, as surely as if
Peter were embracing her.

Laura knelt there for she didn't know how long, not
wanting the moment to end. Finally, however, her knees
began to ache and one leg had fallen asleep, so she swung
her body up onto the couch. It was five thirty; Peter should
be home any time. She prayed that he wouldn't be late;
she had so much to tell him.

She finished reading the Sunday school lesson, marking
the important points with a pink highlighting marker. She
looked at the clock. Six o'clock. She wondered when Peter
would be home.

Finally, as she was putting the Sunday school materials
away in the den, she heard Peter's car in the driveway.
She rushed to the back door.

"Peter, Peter, I had the most incredible experience this
afternoon," she exclaimed, bursting into the kitchen just
as he entered the back door.

"Good grief. What is it, sweetheart?"

"I don't know how to explain it, really. But God healed
me this afternoon."

"I didn't know you were sick."

"Oh, I was. I was terribly sick, but it didn't have anything to do with a fever or a rash. I've been emotionally
sick, sin sick, like the old time preachers used to say."

"Slow down, sweetheart. Now, exactly what are you talking about?"

"I've been feeling so worthless, so useless, so empty lately. It's not a dramatic illness, just a sort of slow interior
rot. Anyway, I was reading the book of Hosea . . . "

"Any particular reason, or did the fancy just strike?"

"It's the Sunday school lesson for this Sunday. I thought
I'd get my lesson ready early."

"You must have been sick."

"Oh, Peter, I'm serious. Very serious," Laura said, laughing. "Anyway, I was reading Hosea and had an almost mystical experience."

"Let's sit down and you tell me from the beginning what happened. I've never seen you this excited," said Peter, leading her into the living room. They sat down on the sofa and Peter held her hands tightly in his.

"It's hard to explain verbally what happened. I've been struggling so much lately. I know God forgives sins and all that—I've had the mechanics of redemption pounded into my head since I was a girl. But lately it just hasn't seemed real in my life."

"I think I know what you mean."

"So I was reading Hosea, and it was talking about how the Israelite people were worshiping other gods and acting like an adulterous wife. And God was angry, horribly angry. It's poetry. It explains how shamefully the people turned their backs on God and how wrathful he felt toward them. But, when they repented, he forgot his anger. He was actually eager to forgive them. He's not a human being, so he can do that. It is so beautiful."

"But how is that different from what you knew all along, that God forgives sins. That's sort of basic Christian knowledge, isn't it?"

"Yes, Peter, but reading Hosea somehow moved me. It talks about God healing the people. That's what I needed. He doesn't stop at just forgiving us, but wants to heal us, too."

"Well, that's sort of part of it, isn't it?"

"Yes, but, Peter, this was a unique experience. I don't want to sound dramatic, but I felt like God was actually, physically here with me."

"Where?"

"Here in our living room. I was kneeling right where we're sitting. I actually felt like God was putting his arm around me to console me. He says in Hosea that he will 'love them'—that is, the people who repent—'freely.' Not dutifully love us, but love us freely. I know this sounds like the same old stuff you always hear, but I'm telling you, Peter, this was different. Am I making any sense at all?"

"Yes, you are. I'm trying to act skeptical because it's my nature, but if I'm honest, I have to admit that I know exactly what you're saying. I've been feeling the same way, too."

"I've been trying to act like a Christian, to be a Christian in my own strength. I've relied on my many warriors and have lost my fortresses."

"That's something out of Hosea, right?"

"Yes, you've got to read it. It's like it was written especially for me. I've never had Scripture affect me like this before."

"The Old Testament, except for maybe Psalms, usually isn't my cup of tea. I'm more of a New Testament person."

"So am I. That's why I was so surprised when this Scripture struck me this way. I wasn't expecting it at all."

Peter took off his suit jacket and tossed it on the overstuffed chair. Laura curled up next to him on the couch.

"Let me read you the passages I highlighted," she suggested, taking their Bible from the coffee table. Peter nodded, and she began reading to him in the still room.

When she had finished, Peter, without saying a word, eased himself off the couch and knelt on the floor. Laura followed him, and together they hid their faces in their hands. Laura sensed rather than heard Peter begin to cry and put her arm around him.

In the silent living room the only other sound was the ticking and occasional chiming of Grandma's clock and the sound of rain on the windows. They prayed and cried together until the room grew dark.

□

"Elaine? Hi! This is Laura. Do you remember me?"

"Laura! It's great to hear from you. I knew you'd call."

"I thought you'd have given up on me. It's been three months since I left."

"Well, that's not very long, really, for getting your life

back together. And from your happy tone of voice, I gather
that's what's happened."

"Well, if you don't mind hearing about a religious experience, I'll tell you all about it sometime."

"Hey, I'm for whatever works. You can tell me everything sometime when I'm not in the middle of a tight deadline, whenever that might be. Business has really picked
up. I've hired two other people to help with keyboarding
and proofreading."

"Oh. Well then you probably won't be needing me . . . "

"Laura, I can always use you. Were you wanting to come
back to work? I figured you'd go crazy being at home."

"Well, yes and no. I mean, I was wondering if there were
any way I could work on projects for you here at home.
Editing, writing and proofreading projects are all quite
portable."

"That's a great idea. I could definitely use some help
with the overflow editing and copywriting. The people I've
hired are good at what they do, but they don't have your
background. But why would you want to work at home?
You aren't pregnant are you?"

"No, unfortunately not. But I've decided what I want to
do, which for me is a marvelous achievement in and of itself."

"What's that?"

"I want to start a business here at home, helping you
and other publishing and out-of-house production firms
handle their overflow work, to help them meet the impos-
sible deadlines they're always setting for themselves."

"Well, you should be able to get plenty of work."

"I figure it will be a good deal for whoever hires me because I'll work on an hourly rate and they won't have to
pay overhead on me—won't have to provide an office, pay
insurance benefits and things like that."

"So you really like working at home?"

"I love being here, but I also love working in my field.
This way, if the moon should turn blue and I do get pregnant I'll already have a home-based business and won't

have to worry about leaving little whomever when the six
week maternity leave is over or about finding competent
day care."

"One part of me thinks you're insane, Laura," said
Elaine. "But another part of me applauds you. I could
never do it—I'd go nuts—but I think it's great that women
are finding some alternatives to either staying at home or
working. We're always trying to fit into job roles that were
defined by men, and they don't fit us any better than a
man's shoes would fit. Part-time work, flextime, working
at home. It's wonderful. The women's movement is finally
starting to help real women improve their lives."

"Well, I'm not part of any movement, Elaine," said
Laura, smiling.

"Yes, you are, Laura. You're what the women's movement is all about. You won't accept a cookie cutter role for
yourself. Anyway, before I get all teary-eyed, let's get down
to business. When do you want to start?"

"ASAP."

"Great. I've just got a huge manuscript in from
Northwest. As usual, they need help meeting some
ridiculous deadline. Anyway, the thing's a mess. The
author quit about half way through and the in-house
editor tried to finish it by revising the previous edition. Except it's one of those manuals for WordPerfect—you know
how Northwest produces instruction manuals for all the
popular word processing programs since the ones that
come with the software are always so inscrutable—and
the new version is quite different and the editor didn't
know what he was doing. You'd be ideal for the job because
you've used the new version and you could catch his mistakes while you edit. Interested?"

"Sounds good to me. I've got the new WordPerfect on my
PC, so I could check out anything that doesn't sound right.
It would be amusing to work for Northwest without
having to go there."

"Why don't you come out this afternoon and we'll go

over the specs for the book, and I'll just dump the entire project in your lap."

"Fine. What time?"

"How about two o'clock. And Laura . . . "

"Yes?"

"Don't worry about contacting any other companies. As busy as we've been, I have no doubt I can give you as much work as you want and then some. I've been swamped lately because I've been taking on more than I can handle. You're a godsend."

"And don't you forget it! I'll be there at two and get all the gory details of what's been happening. It'll be great to see you again."

"Sure will. Laura, you couldn't have called at a better time."

□

When Peter walked through the door that night, he was surprised to find Laura in her navy blue linen suit, best white blouse and silk bow tie sitting at the kitchen table surrounded by an assortment of printouts.

"Well, what have we here?" he asked as he bent over the table to see what she was working on.

"I'm back in the saddle again," Laura bubbled. "I swallowed my pride and called Elaine, and she's given me an entire project right off the bat. This manuscript is a disaster."

"Oh. So you'll be working out there again," Peter said, unbuttoning his navy blue suit coat.

"Not exactly. I'm going to be working at home and just go out there once or twice a week as needed to pick up and drop things off. Or, if we're really busy, I'll just use courier services to get stuff back and forth."

"So you'll be working at home. That's wonderful. That'll work out perfectly when we have a baby."

"Precisely. Oh, Peter, why didn't I think of this before? You see, I've enjoyed being at home, but I've missed working, too. This way I have the best of both worlds."

"This is the best of all possible worlds, sweetheart. Hey, let's celebrate by eating out someplace nice tonight."

"You could talk me into that," smiled Laura.

"And, something else I was thinking we might do tonight."

"Yes . . . "

"Well, you know the new Bible study the minister has started in his home on Thursdays?"

"Yes . . . "

"Well, this is Thursday. Maybe that would be a good thing for us to go to together. What do you think?"

"I think that you are the most wonderful husband in the universe," said Laura, as she stood up and hugged Peter, their bodies forming one solid mass of navy blue suit.

Chapter 13

Home Again, Home Again, Jiggidy Jig

□ ■ □

It was ten thirty in the morning on July 23, a Tuesday. Laura was sitting at the library table, drinking her second cup of capuccino and poring over the problem-filled manuscript. She pushed herself away from the desk for a moment and stretched.

It's all starting to run together. I think I'd better take a quick break, she thought as she pushed the massive print-out away. Looking at the telephone on the desk, she had an idea. She found her red address book in the library table drawer, looked up a number and began dialing.

"Hello, Aunt Naomi? This is Laura Morton."

"Hi Laura. Thank you so much for the gorgeous birthday card."

"Oh, great. I was calling to make sure it arrived on time."

"It certainly did. I was surprised to hear from you again. I thought you'd written me off as a grouchy old woman."

"Of course not. I would've called you sooner, but I've been busy lately. I've started back to work, sort of. I'm working at home, just making a trip once or twice a week

to the office to drop off or pick up assignments. How are
you celebrating your birthday?"

"Well, two of my nieces came over last night and fixed
me a birthday supper. Amber, she's twelve, and Kim, who's
fourteen. We had a wonderful time. They're Frank's
sister's girls. They live out in Blue Ash."

"So they got you to celebrate early."

"They couldn't come over tonight because Kim has gym-
nastics practice—she's really good—and Amber had a soc-
cer game."

"Do you have any plans for tonight?"

"No, I guess not. Birthdays aren't what they used to be
since Frank's gone. He always made such a fuss over
them. But then I'm at the age where I'd just as soon not
remember how many birthdays I've had anyway."

"Well, we'd love to have you over tonight, if you'd like to
come. You only live twenty minutes away; I can come get
you while Peter fixes dinner. He's dying to meet you."

"Your husband fixes dinner?"

"He's a liberated man, Aunt Naomi. Lately I've been
doing most of the cooking because I have more time, but
he's a better cook than I am."

"Oh, I don't want to put you to any bother."

"It's no bother at all. It'd be so much fun."

"Well, if you're sure it's no trouble. It would be nice to
see you again. I enjoyed our first visit."

"Aunt Naomi."

"Yes, Laura."

"I just had another splendid idea, but I don't know what
you'll think about it."

"What is it?"

"How would you feel if I invited Grandma over for din-
ner, too? I know you said you didn't want to meet her, and
I'd understand if you didn't want me to bring her over, but
I thought I'd ask in case you'd reconsidered."

"Well, I appreciate your asking instead of just springing
it on me and inviting her without telling me. I have been
thinking about what you said. I don't hate your

grandmother. How could I hate my own mother? But I feel
a lot of resentment for what she did. On the other hand,
she gave me life. It's not like women never had abortions
in those days. I've had a full and wonderful life, and I
guess I do owe your grandmother that. Yes, Laura, if you
really think she wants to see me, invite her."

"I'm sure she will. I'm so glad you agreed. We'll all
celebrate your birth tonight."

"I suppose she was there when I was born so it's a fitting time for me to meet her. You won't tell your mother or
anyone else in the family about me, though, will you? I
don't know if I'm up to meeting all of them. It will take all
the emotional energy I've got just to confront your
grandmother."

"I promise I won't tell anyone. I'll tell Mom that we're
having a friend over whom Grandma might like to get to
know. I'll be there to pick you up about five o'clock, if that's
okay."

"That's fine."

"I can't wait to see you again, Aunt Naomi. Thanks for
accepting our invitation."

"Oh, no, thank you."

"See you tonight."

□

As Laura hung up the phone, she had a horrible
thought. *What if Grandma doesn't want to meet Aunt
Naomi? Or what if she really doesn't remember anything
about that baby—her memory isn't what it used to be. I
may have created a terrible situation. How awful if Aunt
Naomi were to be rejected by her mother a second time in
her life. And it would all be my fault for butting my nose in
where it doesn't belong. When fools rush in, I always lead
the pack. Act first, think later . . . that's my motto.*

With dread, Laura called her parents' home.

"Hi, Mom? This is Laura."

"Laura! How good to hear from you."

"Mom, I was wondering. We're having an older lady over

tonight to celebrate her birthday. She's a widow and would be celebrating alone otherwise. Anyway, this woman is from West Virginia, and I thought it would be great to have Grandma over, too. They might have a lot in common."

"Honey, how old is this widow friend of yours?"

"In her sixties, I guess."

"Well, your grandmother is old enough to be her mother. They probably won't have much in common. That would be like you being at a party for a three year old."

"I know they're from different generations, but they're both from rural West Virginia and they are both adults. Besides, I thought Grandma might like to get out. It would give you and Dad an evening alone, too."

"Honey, we're past the age where we need an evening alone together, believe me."

"Well, maybe I could talk to Grandma and ask her if she'd like to come over tonight. I'll come and pick her up."

"You know your grandma has a hard time hearing on the telephone. Anyway, I don't think it's a good idea, sweetheart."

"But I think she'd enjoy getting out." *Why does Mom act like she's Grandma's keeper? This is ridiculous.*

"I don't think you understand how much work it is taking your grandmother places. We don't have a ramp for her wheelchair so she has to be carried in and out of the house. You know she can't control her bowels anymore and has to wear those adult diapers."

"Peter and I can take care of getting her in the car and in and out of the house. We're not talking about an overnight trip, just a meal at our house."

"That's why it doesn't seem worth it, dear."

"Please, Mom."

"Well, okay. But don't say I didn't warn you when everything ends in disaster. And she's a picky eater, too. What are you having?"

"I thought we'd have lasagna because I can get it all

ready ahead of time and we'll just have to make the salads at the last minute."

"Well, she'll never eat lasagna."

"Have you ever made it?"

"No. Your father's strictly a meat and potatoes man."

"Then how do you know Grandma won't eat it?"

"I just know she won't."

"Well, I'll think about it. Maybe I'll make something else. Anyway, Peter and I will be over about three thirty to get her."

"My, Peter's getting off early tonight. When did Tuesday night become so special?"

"He's just going to take a few hours of vacation time he has coming to him."

"Well, I'll have Grandma ready to go then."

"Thanks, Mom."

Rats. I wanted to talk to Grandma first to make sure she really wanted to come meet her long lost daughter. And what if Peter can't get off early today? Maybe I have romanticized this whole mother-child relationship. Maybe they're just two grown women with nothing to say to each other. As usual, I've made a mess of things.

The next task was to call Peter.

"Hello. This is Laura Morton. May I speak to Peter Morton?"

"One moment, please."

Laura doodled in the margin of the manuscript as she endured a tinny rendition of "The Sound of Silence."

"Hi, Laura. What's up?"

"Peter, I need you to do me the biggest favor."

"What is it, sweetheart?"

"Can you get off work early today?"

"I don't know. Why?"

"Well, I sort of on the spur of the moment invited Aunt Naomi over for dinner tonight. It's her birthday and she was going to be all alone tonight."

"That's great. But why do I need to get off early?"

"Well, I also invited Grandma over. We need to go get

her about three thirty in order to get her here and give me
time to go get Aunt Naomi in Cleves. It'll take both of us to
get Grandma from the house to the car and then from the
car to our house."

"The mother and child reunion. That's great. What did
your grandma say when she found out she'd be meeting
her youngest child?"

"I didn't have a chance to talk to her yet."

"She doesn't know? You're just going to spring it on her?
That isn't very nice, is it?"

"I didn't have any choice. I sort of spontaneously asked
Aunt Naomi if she minded if Grandma were at dinner
tonight, and she said she wouldn't mind. Then when I
called to invite Grandma, I got Mom of course. I couldn't
let her know what's up because I promised Aunt Naomi I
wouldn't, and Mom wasn't going to bring Grandma to the
phone."

"What are you going to do if Grandma doesn't want to
meet Aunt Naomi?"

"Well, I figure we'll talk to Grandma in the car and take
it from there. Anyway, can you get off early?"

"Somehow. I'll leave about three o'clock."

"Thanks, Peter. See you then."

□

Peter walked in the back door at three-fifteen, greeted
by the smells of lasagna and Pine Sol.

"I hope the place looks presentable," said Laura. "I did
some last minute cleaning. I haven't been keeping up with
the housework since I've been working again."

"It looks fine. But I don't think anybody is going to be
looking for dust with all the emotional fireworks
scheduled for tonight."

"I know I've botched things up. Let's get going and try to
salvage a Kodak moment out of all this."

Laura and Peter drove to her parents' home, where
Laura's grandmother was waiting. Laura's mother had

packed a tote bag full of extra socks and sweaters and handkerchiefs.

"Well, this sure is a surprise!" crowed Grandma happily as Laura and Peter helped her into the Honda. *If she only knew just how much of a surprise*, thought Laura.

Laura had intended to discuss the situation with Grandma as they rode in the car, but the traffic was too loud to communicate with Grandma, who was slightly hard of hearing. When they reached Laura and Peter's house and Grandma was settled in the living room, Laura sat down next to her for a quick talk.

"This house puts me to mind of my old place in Toledo," said Grandma as she looked about appreciatively.

"I know. It reminds me of that house a little, too," said Laura. "I think that's why I like this house so much. We kids always had so much fun when we visited you."

"Boys, we sure did."

"Remember how you used to fry us as much bacon as we could eat for breakfast?"

"Yes. Your mother didn't like it, but you was my grand-daughter and I wanted you to eat as much as you wanted."

"Mom had a rule that we could only have three pieces. That's one thing I liked about your house. Mom's rules never applied there."

"We had some fun in that house."

"Grandma, I have to tell you something. I hope I haven't done something stupid. I don't know how to tell you this. . ."

"What is it, honey?"

"I found out that you had a daughter just before you left West Virginia. Her name is Naomi, and she lives near here. Today is her birthday and I'm having her over for a birthday dinner, and I thought you might want to see her again after all these years. I wanted to tell you before I dragged you over here, in case you didn't want to see her, but I couldn't tell you without going through Mom, and Aunt Naomi didn't want me to tell Mom or anyone else but you about her."

Grandma didn't say anything. She stared at Laura
blankly, her eyes starting to glisten.

"I'm supposed to leave now to go get her for dinner. If
you don't want to see her, Peter and I will take you home
first. It's up to you. I hope I haven't caused you any heart-
ache, Grandma."

Grandma didn't say anything for a few moments. Laura
hung her head, her own eyes beginning to burn with tears.

Finally, Grandma answered in a low voice, "I've prayed
for this day for over sixty years. Yes, go fetch her."

"That's fantastic, Grandma. I'll wheel you into the
kitchen where you can keep Peter company as he makes
the salads and the garlic bread and ices the birthday cake.
She lives about twenty minutes away, so I'll be back in less
than an hour."

□

Her heart singing, Laura pulled into her Aunt Naomi's
driveway and walked up to the door of the neat little cape
cod house. She didn't have to ring the bell because Aunt
Naomi met her at the door.

As they drove back to Price Hill, Laura noticed that
Aunt Naomi kept nervously tying and untying a flowered
scarf around her neck.

"Grandma was really thrilled to be meeting you tonight.
When I told her you were coming, she said she'd prayed
for this day for over sixty years."

"Laura, I don't mean to be rude, but let's please not
delve into that. My response to that would be, 'Well why
didn't you come back for me when I was a child if you
wanted to see me so badly?' This is not going to be one of
those sentimental type reunions. I'm just meeting her to
try to get some peace about the whole situation and maybe
to find out why she did it."

"So tell me about your life as a doctor's wife," said
Laura, quickly changing the subject.

"Hah. It was wonderful, but it's not easy being married
to a physician. Especially back when doctors made house

calls. He got away from that near the end of his practice, but he would still go visit some of his older patients when they called. And did people ever call, any time of the day or night. One Christmas Eve . . . "

When the much too quick twenty minute trip ended and they pulled into Laura and Peter's driveway, Aunt Naomi became very quiet. As they walked into the kitchen, Peter was bustling around with last minute details of the meal while Grandma sat, looking very small and very old, in her wheelchair behind the kitchen table.

"Aunt Naomi, this is my husband, Peter," said Laura, gesturing to Peter, who was washing lettuce at the sink.

"Hi! Nice to meet you," said Peter, turning around and smiling at them.

"And this," said Laura as she walked around the table and took her grandmother's hand, "is my grandma."

"How do you do," said Aunt Naomi, extending her hand and dashing Laura's hopes for a warm, tearful embrace.

"Well, I'll be," said Grandma. "So this is my little Naomi. Come set down here and tell me all about yourself."

"There's not much to tell," said Aunt Naomi, looking solemn.

"Peter, I think we'd better get things ready in the dining room," said Laura, motioning to the door with her head.

"Oh, yeah. Good idea, sweetheart," said Peter as he carried a stack of blue willow dishes.

"Laura," said Grandma hesitantly, "why don't you set here and visit with us?"

"Oh, I imagine you two want to be alone," said Laura nervously.

"No, please stay," said Aunt Naomi. "After all, you're the one who got us together tonight."

"Well, if you're sure you want me to," said Laura as she sat slowly in one of the kitchen chairs.

No one said anything for a few moments. Finally, Aunt Naomi sighed and looked at her lap. "Why didn't you come back for me?" she asked without looking at Grandma.

"It was a terrible hot summer. You come early and were

so tiny. I'd had so many babies, but never one as teeny as
you. You fit inside the doctor's hand. The doctor said you
probably wouldn't live and that I shouldn't get attached to
you. You didn't even cry good when you was born."

"Why did you let the doctor take me away?"

"He said he could take care of you better than I could.
He said you'd need special care and you might not ever be
right. He said I couldn't take you to Toledo, that you would
never make it. Things back then wasn't like they are today
with modern medicine and all. I cried because I didn't
know what to do. We'd already settled up selling the
house. I wanted to leave you with some of our kin, but the
doctor said they couldn't take care of you right. He said
he'd take you in and he and his wife would attend you till
you commenced to get better, or until you died."

"But why didn't you come back for me?"

Grandma stared at the oak table top. Tracing the grain
with her bony, swollen jointed finger, she continued her
story. "I wrote to the doctor, Gilbert was his last name . . . "

"Yes, I know."

". . . asking them how you was. They didn't write too
much, but every few months they'd send me a letter or
note. You was sick for a long time, but finally they told me
you was getting better. But they said you was happy there,
and they cared for you like a daughter. They had a big
fancy place and only two little girls of their own. He kept
writing me how it would be so much better for you to stay
with them because they had more money and more room
and because you was so happy there."

"But you were my mother. Didn't you want me back?"

"I wanted you back from the day you was born. But I
thought you was better off living with the doctor's family.
We didn't have nothing, and I didn't have any way to go
back to get you."

"All those years I wondered how my own mother could
give me away."

Grandma was quiet for what seemed like a long time.
Laura squirmed on the hard oak chair.

"Finally, Clyde got to doing better," Grandma continued. "We bought a big house in Toledo. I wrote the doctor and said we would come get you. But he wrote back and said you was much happier where you was and that it would be hard on a little girl to go live with strangers, because, see, we was strangers to you by then. We thought you would be better off if you stayed with them and it wouldn't be right for us to take you away from everything you knowed."

"My father—Dr. Gilbert—never told me you wrote to him about me. I always thought you just gave me up and forgot about me," said Aunt Naomi slowly.

"There never has been a day gone by that I haven't thought about my baby. I prayed and prayed that God would let me see you before I died, and praise him, he has."

Aunt Naomi reached out and took Grandma's hand in hers. Laura avoided looking at them by staring at the cut glass jelly dish in the center of the table.

The three women sat there a few moments without saying anything.

"I think I smell something burning," said Naomi suddenly, wrinkling her nose.

"Oh, my goodness. I smell it, too," said Laura, jumping up and running to the oven. "It's just a little of the tomato sauce that boiled over. The lasagna is ready. Shall we eat?"

As Peter rounded up the meal, Laura and Aunt Naomi maneuvered Grandma's wheelchair into the dining room. They placed her at the head of the table, which was covered with a white damask tablecloth and set with Laura's blue willow dishes.

"Grandma, would you say grace for us?" Laura asked.

Grandma bowed her head. "Oh, Lord, we thank you for these your gifts we are about to receive. We thank you for a loving family. Amen."

"I hope everyone likes lasagna," said Laura as they raised their heads.

"I adore lasagna," said Aunt Naomi as she tore a piece of garlic bread off the loaf Peter was passing.

"I don't know what it is," said Grandma, "but it smells good."

"Here, Aunt Naomi," said Peter as he passed her the steaming casserole. "It's your birthday. You go first."

"Thank you, Peter," said Aunt Naomi as she helped herself to a large portion. "You know, I never cared for my name. But tonight I do feel a little like Naomi, returning home from Moab. Laura, you make me feel so at home, even though this is only the second time we've laid eyes on each other."

"We give you the name Naomi," said Grandma as Laura scooped some lasagna onto her plate. "I always liked that name."

"So, where did you go to church when you lived in West Virginia?" asked Naomi. Laura noticed that her aunt avoided calling Grandma "mother."

"Oh, we used to go to a little Baptist church up on . . . "

□

Later that night, Laura and Peter took Grandma home, with strict instructions not to tell Laura's mother who the honored guest had been. As they drove Naomi home, Laura still wondered if she had done the right thing.

"Aunt Naomi, thank you so much for meeting with Grandma tonight. I know it meant the world to her," said Laura, not wanting to pry but wondering what Aunt Naomi thought of the reunion. She and Grandma had been cordial at dinner and they had hugged each other goodnight, but it hadn't been the overwhelming emotional experience Laura had expected.

"Well, Laura, you certainly made this the most unusual birthday of my life. I can't say all my resentment against your grandmother is gone, because I still think she could have done more to find me when I grew older. But I feel more peace about my childhood than I ever have in my life, and for that I thank you."

"I was so worried that I had made a terrible mistake," said Laura. "I didn't want to interfere in either of your

lives, but I thought that deep down you two would want to
see each other, no matter what had happened."

"You didn't make a mistake. You were trying to be a
peacemaker. I know a lot of my problem was of my own
making. When I was a child, I blamed all my troubles on
the fact that I was abandoned at birth, even when they
were just the normal difficulties of growing up. Through
Opal, I could have contacted your grandma myself, but instead I chose to hold a grudge, which is not the Christian
thing to do. Part of me always wanted to find her, but
another part of me was afraid to."

They were pulling into Aunt Naomi's driveway. "Happy
birthday, Aunt Naomi," said Laura.

"It has been a happy day," Naomi replied.

Laura walked her aunt to her front door while Peter
waited in the car.

"Thank you for coming over tonight, Aunt Naomi."

"Thank you for having me, Laura. The lasagna and
everything else was delicious."

"Thanks. Grandma even liked it, though Mom was sure
she wouldn't touch it."

"I was amazed that a woman her age could eat something like that. Guess we're never too old to try something
new."

"Grandma eats anything she likes. I know people my
age who can't do that. She's an amazing woman."

"Good night, Laura, and thank you." Aunt Naomi smiled
and went into her well-tended little house.

Back in the car, Laura sighed as she buckled her seat
belt.

"The big reunion wasn't quite what I thought it would
be."

"It could have been worse," observed Peter as he backed
into the deserted street. "They could have yelled at each
other."

"I think they really do love each other. Otherwise, they
wouldn't have agreed to the get-together. I know Grandma

loves her daughter. But Aunt Naomi has years of hurt feelings to get over."

"It takes time for love to mature," said Peter. "I mean, look at us. When we got married, I thought I loved you as much as I possibly could. But compared to today, my love for you then was nothing."

"That's odd, because then you didn't know all the rotten stuff about me that you know today."

"Ah, but you didn't know the rotten stuff about me, either. Actually, I think that's the point. Until you know all the ugly things about the other person, you're really only loving a figment of your own imagination. Now that we've been married seven years . . . "

"Almost eight."

" . . . we know a lot more about each other and yet we're still in love. We are in love, aren't we?"

"Completely, totally and hopelessly."

Chapter 14

Noel

□ ■ □

"Let's have a Christmas party this year," suggested
Laura one chilly November evening as she and Peter
worked in the dining room. Peter was poring over some
large, unwieldy sales reports while pieces of artwork and
pasteup sheets covered Laura's half of the table.

"Where did you get that idea, honey?" Peter asked
without looking up from his work.

"We haven't had a party in ages. It just seems like the
thing to do. It would be fun to get the house all decorated
and bake a lot of cookies . . . "

"Are you going to do this in your spare time, dear?"

"Of course it will be a lot of work, but it'll be fun, too.
This is going to be the best Christmas ever, and I want to
share it with everyone we know."

"We're going to invite everyone we know?"

"Why not? It'll be a multi-generational party like the
ones Mom had when I was a kid. We'll have different
games and activities going on in different rooms, and
people can wander around and eat and talk and choose
what they want to do. We'll make a big fire in the fireplace
and fill the house with candles . . . "

"You know, I didn't think I'd ever hear you say you were
going to have a wonderful Christmas until you were preg-

nant. Last year certainly wasn't very jolly, as I recall. You
were depressed the entire holiday season."

"Well, I'm still disturbed about being barren . . . "

"Quit using that word!"

" . . . but I have so much to be thankful for—work that I
enjoy, a beautiful home, a loving family, you. We are so
blessed, Peter."

"You know," said Peter thoughtfully, "I used to worry
that I wasn't enough for you. You were so obsessed with
having a baby. I wanted one, too, but even if we never had
children I knew I could live with that. I was afraid you
couldn't."

"I've done a lot of thinking these last few months.
Seeing how God answered Grandma's prayers after sixty
some years really opened my eyes. Who am I to second
guess his timing? When we studied the prophets in my
Sunday school class last summer I began realizing how ungrateful I am. No matter how much God did for me, it
wasn't enough. He gave me miraculous manna and I
whined for quail. When the prophets talked about stiff-
necked people, they meant me."

"Speaking of that little pile of monsters, are you wanting to invite your Sunday school kids to this party?"

"Of course. This is going to be the biggest and best
Christmas party in recorded history."

□

On Friday, December 23, Laura and Peter's house
looked so festive it could have been the cover of *Better
Homes and Gardens*. A delicate snow had fallen and glis-
tened in the light from their windows. A mammoth pine
wreath with an immense red bow covered their front door.
Luminaries, candles sitting in paper bags with snowflake
designs punched in them, outlined their sidewalk and led
to their front porch. Cars were everywhere, cramming the
driveway and lining both sides of the street.

Laura, stunning in a black velvet skirt, ivory silk blouse
and a corsage of small red poinsettia leaves, greeted

guests at the door and steered them to the dining room
table heaped with holiday goodies. Peter worked the
crowd, smiling his wonderful crinkly smile like a youthful
Santa Claus, carrying coats to the guest room and making
swift introductions right and left. People filled every room
of the house and even sat on the steps balancing plates of
cookies and glasses of punch or hot cider.

"Sharon, I'm so glad you and Chuck could make it back
to God's country for Christmas," said Laura, hugging her
friend as she entered the door.

"Something about the idea of spending Christmas in
New Jersey just doesn't get it, does it?" laughed Sharon.

"Actually, we came back here so we could do our
Christmas shopping cheap," added Chuck, smiling.
"There's Peter. I've got to go extract a promise from him
that he'll take some vacation time to come visit us next
year. I'm taking some time off now, and it isn't killing me
at all."

As Chuck strode through the crowd, Laura bent close to
Sharon's ear. "How is everything going? I've been thinking
about you two so much."

"Fine, just fine. And I really mean it. We're in the
process of adopting a special needs child, so we're extremely excited about that. We decided that maybe God was
trying to tell us something."

"How's your relationship with Chuck going? Believe me,
I know what a strain worrying about infertility can place
on a marriage."

"We're closer now than ever before. It was really weird.
It was like God was speaking to both of us at the same
time about adopting a child who really needs us. Although
we'd never discussed it, we each came up with the idea on
our own. It's given us a sense of purpose and helps us
make sense of some of the craziness in the world."

"Do you know what kind of child you're going to adopt?"

"They're not through with the paperwork on us yet, but
if all goes well, by next spring we'll be the parents of a five-
year-old girl named Karen. She has Down Syndrome and

has lived with a lot of foster families. She has the most delightful spirit. We can't wait until she can live with us."

"I'm so happy for you, Sharon. Think how much fun you'll have next Christmas watching her open her packages."

"I can't wait. Is anyone else from the old college gang here tonight?"

"Pat's here with her husband, Tom. She was in the den playing Pictionary last time I saw her. Guess what. She had a little girl on Thanksgiving day; they named her Clara. And this month they're moving into a gorgeous new house in Villa Hills. We went out to eat with them last weekend and they took us through it. Can you believe she didn't even want to be pregnant?"

"Of course she didn't. How else could she have gotten pregnant? But I'm sure she's thrilled now that the baby's here."

"Oh, she is. The baby is a doll."

"Well, I'll go see if I can find her and quit hogging the hostess for awhile. It's so good to see you, Laura."

"Same here," said Laura, hugging Sharon again.

No sooner had Laura handed Sharon and Chuck's coats to Peter than Nancy and Michael appeared at the door.

"Ding dong," said Nancy as Laura opened the front door before they had a chance to ring the bell.

"Thanks so much for coming," exclaimed Laura. "We haven't seen you since last Labor Day. How's everything?"

"Great," said Nancy. "I had the most incredible experience two days ago. Rosalie, my client, remember I told you about her, had her baby last Wednesday at two twenty-five in the morning, and I was her labor coach. I still haven't come down to earth."

"And you still haven't quit talking about it," said Michael, smiling.

"I know, but it was so fantastic. Everything went perfectly. It was a textbook delivery. She had a little boy and named him Nathan, after her father. You know, I never thought I'd say this," Nancy continued, looking sideways

at Michael with a twinkle in her dark eyes, "but it almost
makes me think I might want to be a mother some day."

"I would think witnessing someone go through labor
would make you give that idea up forever," laughed Laura.

"To be honest, that part wasn't too appealing," Nancy
replied. "But I'll never forget the look on Rosie's face. I
mean, she was a mess—exhausted and sweaty and all
that. But I've never seen anything that close to pure joy."

"I hope she still has that look after she's changed her
one thousandth diaper," snickered Michael.

"Oh, Michael, you're such a realist. Laura, where's the
punch? I led a seminar all day today and my throat is dry
from talking so much."

"She constantly has a sore throat," teased Michael, putting his arm around Nancy's plump shoulders.

"The refreshments are in the dining room. It's help yourself, buffet style. There are two kinds of fruit punch, hot
spiced cider, coffee—regular and decaf—and hot water for
tea."

"I don't know, honey, do you think we'll be able to find
anything we like?" asked Michael with a chuckle as they
moved through the crowd.

Since no one was coming up the walk, Laura left her
post at the front door and began to mingle. *I hope everyone
is having a good time. We invited such an odd assortment
of people—but it seems to be working.* In the kitchen,
Elaine's two children and Aunt Naomi's nieces were sitting
around the round oak table, making Christmas ornaments
with glue, glitter and old Christmas cards. Laura's
grandmother's wheelchair was in one corner, and Laura's
mother and Aunt Opal stood on either side of her, balancing plates of cookies and punch glasses. Elaine was lean-
ing against the kitchen counter.

"Laura, I just can't get over our new addition to the
family," said Laura's mother as Laura entered the kitchen.

"That's such a bizarre story. Imagine finding out you
have a sibling you never knew existed," said Elaine. "I'm
taking notes for my great American novel."

"Thanks so much for coming, Aunt Naomi," said Laura.

Naomi smiled. "You know, Laura, I just learned that
your mother and I have had the same doctor for years. We
might have seen each other in the waiting room and not
known we were sisters."

"Isn't that strange?" said Laura's mother. "Oh, honey,
please help me keep an eye on your father. He's been stuff-
ing himself at your buffet. If you see him, tell him he'd better take it easy on that cheese ball."

"Now, Mom, what kind of hostess nags her guests about
how much they're eating? This is the holidays. Everyone
has my permission to make pigs of themselves at my
house tonight."

Everyone laughed. Laura's mother gave her one of her
patented disapproving smirks where one corner of her
mouth went up and the other down.

Laura flitted into the dining room to see how the
refreshments were holding out. Everything still looked
good. Mrs. Luebbers and Mrs. Busmeyer were hovering
near the table talking to three women from the Thursday
night Bible study Laura and Peter had attended the last
few months. Laura smiled and waved at them on her way
to the front door. She thought she had heard the doorbell
ring through the loud chatter of voices and the Christmas
music coming from their compact disc player in the living
room.

On the way to the front door, she peeked into the den.
The Pictionary players and their spectators had become
quite animated. Her sister-in-law Caroline was watching
the proceedings, holding her one-month-old son, Roger Jr.,
over her shoulder. Laura saw that he was sound asleep,
oblivious to the rise and fall of voices in the small room.
She paused a moment to marvel at his perfect little eye-
lashes and tightly curled fists before resuming her journey
to the front door.

Looking through the beveled glass, Laura saw a band of
youngsters coming up her front walk. *Wonderful! They
came after all, even though Tony said it would be boring.*

She opened the door, exclaiming, "Judy, Heather, Tony, Scott, Kristen! It's great to see you. Merry Christmas!"

"It ain't Christmas, yet," said Scott.

"Hey, where's the food?" shrieked Tony.

"Everything's in the dining room. I'll give you the grand tour of the house and lead you to the refreshments."

"It's so pretty," said Judy.

"Yeah, this is a neat place, Laura," observed Kristen.

"Your Christmas tree is wonderful," Judy added, looking at the huge decorated pine tree beside the crackling fire in the fireplace. "We just have a little artificial one."

"So do we," said Scott sadly. "I keep telling my mom that we need a real Christmas tree, but she says they're too much trouble."

"All Christmas trees are beautiful, even artificial ones," said Laura. "Besides, not too many more years and you guys will be out of college and on your own and can have any kind of Christmas tree you want."

"Yeah. When I get my own apartment, I'm going to decorate a cactus for Christmas. I'll hang ornaments on all the little sticky things," said Scott.

"You're so gross," said Kristen.

"Now, a no-making-fun-of-anyone rule is in effect at this Christmas party. Scott's idea is very creative . . . ," said Laura as she handed the kids' coats to Peter and lead them through the house.

□

The next day was Christmas Eve. Laura and Peter woke up about ten in the morning. As Laura moseyed downstairs to make some coffee, she smiled as she surveyed the mess from the night before. Plastic punch cups and crumb-filled napkins covered nearly every surface.

"Now I wish we'd done some of the clean up last night," said Peter as he came down the stairs behind her. "But I was too exhausted when Sharon and Chuck left at two a.m. to even pick up a toothpick."

"I know what you mean. But it was so good to see them again, it was worth it. Wasn't it a wonderful party, Peter?"

"I was expecting a total disaster, what with inviting such a hodgepodge of people—friends from school, friends from work, relatives, neighbors, people from church, kids—but it all worked out great." He pulled Laura close to him as she paused in the living room to look at the ashes in the fireplace. "Hey, I'll take care of this mess. I know you have to keep up the tradition."

"What tradition?"

"The shopping-at-the-absolute-last-minute tradition."

"Well, there were a few little things I still wanted to get before tomorrow."

"I knew it," said Peter, picking Laura up in a big bear hug.

□

This is probably the very last line I will stand in this shopping season, thought Laura as she waited to have her purchases rung up by a languid department store clerk. She'd found a snow globe with an angel in it that played "Joy to the World" for Grandma and a pair of jade earrings her mother would love. Her eyes swept over the crowded store where people, mostly women, rooted urgently through sloppy racks of clothing and dwindling piles of merchandise on large tables.

Then she noticed a nearby rack of beautiful, tiny garments. *Oh, my goodness. I completely forgot about Caroline's new baby. Of course it, I mean he, wasn't on my gift list from last year. Thank heaven I remembered the poor little guy in time, although I don't suppose he would be traumatized at being forgotten by his aunt and uncle at age one month.*

Laura began flipping through the darling little one-piece outfits hanging on the rack. *The outfits for little girls sure are cute, with all the ruffles and bows. But they're making baby boys' clothes a lot cuter these days, too. This choo choo train outfit is perfect for little Roger Jr. A lot of*

*these would be great for baby shower gifts because they
could be used for either a boy or a girl. This one with the
sleepy moon face on the front is adorable. Hmmmmm . . . I
could get this and keep it for our little whoever, just in case.
No, better not. Maybe that's not part of the plan. I'll have
plenty of time to shop for baby clothes if that day ever
comes.*

Laura returned to the line, dismayed to find it even
longer than when she'd left it. *Rats. I can't wait to get
home to Peter. You know, Lord, thanks to you, I think I am
finally turning the corner on some of my self-centeredness.
Here I am buying a precious little outfit for someone else's
baby and I don't feel anger or jealousy, just love for the
cute, new little guy in our family. I get to be somebody's
aunt. That's nothing to complain about. I can't wait to
start spoiling him. I guess I can do all things through
Christ who strengthens me. Thank you, Lord, for freeing
me from that miserable bitterness and hate.*

Preoccupied with her silent prayer, Laura almost didn't
notice that it was her turn to present her merchandise to
the weary clerk.

□

Late that night, Christmas Eve, Laura and Peter made
a fire in their fireplace and turned off all the other lights.
They sat on the oriental rug in the living room drinking
cocoa and staring at the flickering flames. Magic and
Samantha were curled into neat little balls on the overstuffed chair, purring like little toy engines.

"The Christmas Eve service was beautiful this year."

"I think it was the best one our church has ever had.
That was a neat idea Reverend Tyson had to have
everyone join hands around the sanctuary and hold
candles and sing 'Silent Night' at the end."

"It gave me chills. That's what Christmas is all about. I
was glad most of my Sunday school kids were there."

They sat gazing silently at the fire for a few moments.

"Thanks for giving me extra marshmallows," said Peter, smiling.

"Well of course I'm going to indulge my favorite husband on Christmas Eve, although I couldn't stand to drink it with that many marshmallows. I don't see how you can taste the chocolate," Laura replied as she smoothed her flowered flannel nightgown over her knees.

"Ah . . . that's my favorite way to drink cocoa," said Peter, who was wearing a long, red flannel nightshirt. The foam from the melted marshmallows made a white mustache above his lip.

"You look like a civilian Santa Claus," laughed Laura, touching his frothy white mustache and then licking her finger.

"You've been a good little girl this year," said Peter in his best Santa voice. "Tell old Mr. Claus what you want and maybe it'll be what I already bought for you."

"You've already given me everything I ever wanted, Peter. I couldn't ask for any more."

"I love you, Laura," said Peter as he took Laura's up-turned freckled face in his large hands and kissed her gently. The fire crackled merrily on the hearth as Laura and Peter embraced.

□

The next morning, Laura woke up with that little breathless feeling in her throat that she had always had on Christmas morning. *I may be thirty years old, but Christmas morning is still Christmas morning,* she thought as she started to get up.

Suddenly she remembered that she hadn't taken her temperature yet. *It's so hard to remember to do this every day. I suppose I could skip it since it's Christmas. Oh well, it should be going up soon. I'd better record it just in case.* She reached under the bed for her digital thermometer and put it under her tongue. When she took it out she noticed that her temperature had risen sharply since the day before.

"Any action on the thermometer scene?" asked Peter, who was slowly waking up.

"Yes, it's gone up."

"Well, that's a good sign. Should be good timing after last night."

"True, but we've had good timing a lot of months and nothing has happened. We even used that ovulation prediction kit and supposedly timed it perfectly and nothing happened. So I'm not getting my hopes up."

"Still, it's a good sign. I'll race you to the Christmas tree!" shouted Peter, springing out of bed and running down the stairs like a boy.

"No fair, you got a head start," yelled Laura, bounding out of bed and taking the stairs two at a time.

When they reached the bottom of the steps, they collapsed on the floor and rolled around under the tree, laughing and hugging each other.

"Look, I got just what I wanted!" exclaimed Peter as he looked into Laura's eyes.

"So did I. What a Christmas," Laura answered.

□

On the morning of Saturday, January 15, Laura dutifully groped for the thermometer under the bed and took her temperature before getting up. *This could be the last time I ever have to do that,* she thought as she recorded the temperature on the chart she kept in her top dresser drawer.

"Well, is it still high?" asked Peter, who was lying on his side, propped up on one elbow.

"Sure is," said Laura, not wanting to get too excited. She'd been late so many times before. "I'm going to go get the kit."

She walked down the hall to the bathroom and took the small box from the medicine chest over the sink. She had read and reread the instructions the night before and went through the steps quickly.

"There. Now one of the little marbles is supposed to turn blue within fifteen minutes if it's positive."

"Let's leave it alone for at least ten minutes. You know how we always imagine it's starting to turn blue or pink or whatever right away and get all worked up. Come on, let's get dressed," Peter suggested gently.

"Okay," said Laura, longingly eyeing the plastic stand containing the two beads. "We'll let it sit five minutes before we check."

Back in their bedroom, she went through the motions of getting her clothes out of her closet, keeping her eyes on their alarm clock.

"It's been five minutes," she told Peter, who was fully dressed and straightening his tie.

"And I used to think Christmas morning was exciting," said Peter.

They walked with forced calmness down the hall to the bathroom. Laura bent down to get a good look at the tiny beads in their holder on the vanity countertop.

"Oh, Peter, it's already blue, blue, a beautiful blue!" she screamed.

"Let me see," he said, eagerly bending over the small plastic object. "You're right, it's as blue as blue can be!"

They danced and hugged. Laura cried. Peter started making up a silly song about babies to the tune of "Anchors Away." Laura kept going back to look at the beads over and over again.

"It really was the best Christmas ever," said Laura, her glistening eyes fixed on the beautiful blue marble.